EINSTEIN

EINSTEIN

Louis de Broglie, *Nobel Prize Laureate*,
Louis Armand *of the French Academy*,
Pierre-Henri Simon *of the French Academy*,
et al

Peebles Press
New York/London

This Edition first published 1979 by
PEEBLES PRESS INTERNATIONAL, INC.
10 Columbus Circle, New York, New York 10019

Original French text © Hachette 1966.

English Translation © 1979 Peebles Press International, Inc.
ISBN 0-85690-070-2
Library of Congress Catalog Card Number 78-055393

Graphic Production by Filmar Graphics,
San Diego, California 92110

Distributed in the United States by
Farrar, Straus & Giroux
19 Union Square West, New York, New York 10003

Distributed in Canada by
McGraw-Hill Ryerson, Ltd.
330 Progress Avenue
Scarborough, Ontario

Distributed in the United Kingdom and British Commonwealth by
David & Charles, Ltd.
Brunel House
Newton Abbot
Devon, England

Printed and bound in the United States of America

CONTENTS

EINSTEIN

CHAPTER ONE

A Modest Genius

by JACQUES MADAULE

Albert Einstein was born on March 14, 1879 in Ulm, Wurtemberg, on the Danube. The following year his family left Ulm for Munich. It is important to bear Einstein's Swabian origin in mind, as all his family came from Swabia, and as a matter of fact he continued to freely use their dialect in everyday conversation until the end of his life. His mother was born in Cannstadt, outside of Stuttgart; his father Hermann managed a small electrical equipment business. They were both Jewish, but detached from the religious practices of their people. However, the Einsteins neither denied their origin nor their tradition. At home the Bible was assiduously read along with the works of Lessing, Heine, and Schiller — whom the family particularly worshipped — and other masterpieces of German literature.

In Munich, Einstein attended a Catholic school and there he noticed the profound resemblances between the Jewish traditions that he learned at home and the Catholic traditions that were taught to him in school. To him the differences seemed of little significance. And yet one day the professor of religious instruction, brandishing a large nail before his students, exclaimed "Here is one of the nails that the Jews used to crucify Jesus!" That day the young Einstein received one of the deepest and most painful shocks of his life. He was never to forget it. He was a child of little promise at that time. He was very slow in everything, and learned to talk very late. At school he obstinately refused to do rote excercises, which he considered too tiring to the mind and of no true benefit. However, when he was four years old his father gave him a sailor's compass as a toy. The child spent hours absorbed in the contemplation of the magnetic needle which always infallibly marked the same direction, no matter what side he turned the compass to. For the first time, he found himself in the presence of the mystery of the universe. But it was not a mystery that human intelligence found impossible to penetrate. Einstein as a child was already concentrating on a problem that had to have a solution since someone had been capable of acknowledging. Much later he would say "The compass and the compass alone stays in my memory to this day."

Otherwise the child grew up in an atmosphere of simplicity and moral health. Hermann, his father, loved to take long walks, stopping to eat sausage in a tavern along the way. All his life Einstein never practiced any sports other than walking and sailing. It seemed that he always needed to feel himself in close contact with the Earth. His studies did not continue too brilliantly. His mother complained that he was only interested in the violin. Music was not only a very lively diversion for him, but a necessity; it put his mind in condition for working and inventing. He played, it seems, decently, but was never a virtuoso, in spite of what has been said of him. Einstein had essentially a reflective and meditative mind. Music helped his concentration, creating the climate that he needed; but it belonged to the outside world. The real man was elsewhere.

There was yet another reason for the relative mediocrity of his studies: a strong militarism reigned in the schools of the Second Reich. Knowledge, of whatever kind, was not offered, but imposed. From the time of his high school years in Munich, Einstein retained an indelible horror of militarism. Certainly he was grateful to some of his professors who revealed the grandeur of German literature to him, especially Goethe and Schiller, whom he never stopped reading, but he appreciated neither history nor geography, and foreign languages even less — especially dead languages, which he accused of uselessly crowding the mind. In mathematics and physics he was, of course, extraordinarily brilliant. He made a distinction in the manuals, between what was fundamental and what was only accessory, the latter which he considered useless to learn because they could always be found in a dictionary if needed. From his childhood on, Einstein was always to orientate himself toward the essential. He was gentle and taciturn, taking only seldom part in the games of his companions and barely speaking to them. At school they called him *Biedermann*, which means a straight and honorable man, one who never lies and would never miss an appointment.

Such was Einstein at fifteen when his father, having had business troubles in Munich, decided to leave Germany and establish himself in Milan, Italy, where he had relatives. Einstein's parents left the young boy in Munich at the home of an old friend who was retired, in order to let Albert finish his studies. He received enthusiastic letters from his mother and his sister Maja in Italy. Abruptly the boy left Munich for Milan. For the first time he had made one of the sudden and irrevocable decisions that were a dominant trait of his character. Einstein was not impulsive. On the contrary, he reflected at length on his decisions, and allowed them to mature. But then he executed them promptly, whatever the difficulties were, and never left anything behind him. It was as if he had no past.

His first contact with Italy enchanted him. There, he found light, art — he was profoundly affected by

Michelangelo's art — and customs that were freer and more open than in his native Germany. He traveled, and walked from Milan to Padua and from there to Florence, Sienna, Perusa and Genoa, where he had relatives. But all of this was hardly in the nature of giving him a job. A family council decided that Albert would go to Zurich to study at the Polytechnic School there. Unfortunately, as he had left Germany without a diploma, he had to take an entrance examination, which he failed. In physics and math he got astonishingly high grades, but he didn't do as well in the classical disciplines. One of his examiners advised him to go to Aarau to improve his languages. There remain few accounts of his stay in Argovia. However it seems that the same way Switzerland was an oasis in Europe for Einstein, Argovia was an oasis for him in Switzerland.

After his return from Aarau he was finally accepted by the Polytechnic School and he studied there for four years, earning his doctorate. He had been promised an assistantship upon his graduation, but the promise wasn't kept. The official reason was that Einstein wasn't a Swiss citizen, but certainly his Jewish origin was of no help either. Furthermore, Einstein had never hesitated to criticize his professors, and some of them, who had sensed his genius, began to be afraid of him. At that point the most materially troubled period of his life began. He would go on for days without eating. One of his fellow students, Marcel Grossmann, who later counted among Einstein's most intimate collaborators, was appalled by this situation and spoke to his father about it. The latter warmly recommended Einstein to a Dr. Haller, who directed a patent office in Bern. Dr. Haller asked Einstein what he knew about patents. "Nothing," Einstein replied, with his usual honesty. But Doctor Haller was an intelligent man. He spoke with the young man for two hours and hired him. From there on his material situation was insured. He was able to acquire Swiss citizenship and he married a young Serbian mathematician, Mileva Maric, whom he had known from the time of his studies at the Polytechnic School. Two sons, Albert and Edward, were born during this first marriage, but it is necessary to understand that Einstein's private life wasn't like anyone else's. It cannot be said that he could not experience normal feelings: he was a good son, a good father and even a good husband in a certain sense; but he never allowed the least interference between his family life and what he considered to be his proper task.

The years in Bern were among the most fruitful in his life. It was in Bern, while he was still employed by the patent office, that he wrote his famous treatise on relativity, which overthrew the foundations of science.* Among the friends in Bern with whom he discussed his researches, was Besso, an engineer, who supported him in moments of self-doubt. For Einstein the birth of the Theory of Relativity was hindered by terrible and painful difficulties. One day he said to a friend, "It is useless for me to continue. I have to give up." It seems that he never spoke of this to his wife. Yet she was a mathematician, and no doubt she would have felt capable of understanding him. But he considered that it was enough for her to organize his material existence somehow or another and take care of their children. We can imagine that Mileva, of whom we know fairly little, was not easily reconciled to such a situation. Yet at that time Einstein had just struck one of those great blows which, in the domain of knowledge, match the discovery of America. All the scientists who got acquainted with his treatise in the *Annals of Physics* were

---

*In Chapter III, "Before Einstein," Theo Kahan gives a portrait of physical science at the dawn of the 20th Century.

overwhelmed.* Von Lau came expressly from Berlin to Bern in order to meet Einstein.

It was right at this moment that Einstein's extraordinary career made its debut. First he was invited to give a speech in Salzburg. Then the famous Lorentz asked Einstein to speak at Leyde University. He was never to forget the quiet university town, nor the attention that was given to him by Lorentz, who was sixty at the time: "With Lorentz, I felt like a student facing his professor." Zurich University offered Einstein a chair. After some hesitation, he accepted because his second son Edouard had just been born, and sixty dollars a month would not be too much for a family to live on. In 1910 he was appointed professor at Prague University, where he taught until 1912. Einstein was very happy in Prague, he seems to have loved the baroque atmosphere and the labyrinth of the old city. But actually he was at home everywhere and nowhere; he never made the least concession to the places where he lived. Finally he got tired of Prague, where Germans and Czechs were in constant conflict and always liable to reconcile their differences on the backs of the Jews. He returned to Zurich, but as a professor at the Polytechnic School where he had earlier been held in contempt.

In reality, whether in Prague, Zurich, or anywhere else, the pursuit of his work was the only thing which essentially engaged his interest. Einstein published articles in the *Annals of Physics* which continually enlarged and deepened the gap which he was opening in traditional physics. His reputation increased world-wide, and hardly had he returned to Zurich when he was visited by Max Planck and Walter

---

*In Chapter IV, "The Relativist Revolution" François le Lionnais analyzes the depth and range of Einstein's scientific contribution.

Nernst, who came on behalf of Emperor Wilhelm II to offer him a chair, without any obligation to teach, at the University of Berlin, and a seat in the Prussian Academy of Science. Einstein, however, did not intend to renounce his Swiss citizenship. The Germans gave in to this demand and thus, in the fall of 1913, less than a year before World War I, Einstein the antimilitarist, the man who had deliberately given up his German citizenship, became a high Prussian official with the rank of Minister of State. But he had, in fact, imposed his own conditions. He said good-bye to Mileva and the two children whom he was leaving with her. He knew that a whole era of his life was over. "It was," as Antonina Vallentin recounts, "perhaps the only time in his life that someone saw him cry."

In Berlin, Einstein at first lived with his uncle, whose daughter Elsa he had known before. He had probably forgotten her, and he found her now mother of two girls, Ilsa and Margot, but in the middle of a divorce, as he himself now was. Quite simply, he married her, in 1915, taking charge of the two girls and left his two sons to Mileva. Elsa Einstein deserves that we spend some time on her because she was the only real, the only true companion to the great scholar in what was to be the most glorious but also, in certain regards, the most difficult and painful period of his life. She was an infinitely discreet and self-effacing woman. She never dreamed of interfering in any of the research which Einstein pursued. She would have been, in any case, unable to cope with it; but she knew how to take perfectly good care of Einstein, and God knows how difficult this was when he truly became a figure of international stature and renown; it then became necessary to filter the flow of visitors who were pressing at the door of their Berlin apartment on Haberlandstrasse. Elsa was extremely myopic and could hardly see the people, but she would almost infallibly guess who they were. She was not however, always in a position to prevent Einstein from welcoming just anyone with that spontaneity, which was one of the dominant traits of his character. She was fond of saying that he hadn't changed since he was a little boy. It was not only necessary to keep an eye on what was happening outside, but also on the great man, who never cared about anything which he didn't judge indispensable. For example, he never knew how to use money and he gave it freely to anyone whom he thought needed it. One day Elsa remarked to him that he had already given to the same fishy character several times. "I know," he answered calmly, "but he still must need the money. He doesn't beg for the pleasure of it." Another time, as he was going out alone, Elsa slipped two dollars into his jacket pocket. The money remained there for a very long time; Einstein had not yet found an opportunity to spend it.

Examples of this nature could be endlessly cited. In reality, Elsa was resigned to these eccentricities and many others as well. She created an atmosphere of good humor around Einstein; she preserved the calm that was indispensable for his reflection; she placed herself as much as possible between her husband and the world. We must certainly thank her in part for the fact that during the most difficult and agitated period of his life, Einstein was able to pursue the research that transformed the world.

He was barely settled in Berlin when the first World War broke out. If Einstein was relatively insensitive to domestic troubles, the great movements of humanity did indeed affect him. In the dark days of July 1914, he witnessed the manifestation of two very different groups in Berlin which were, at the same time, very much alike. The Social Democrats protested "en masse" against the war, but, just a few days later, the Berlin crowd acclaimed the Emperor who had pushed Germany into the war. And this was not only an anonymous group of people, intellectuals, university professors; Einstein's own colleagues at the Prussian Academy also got involved; and ninety-three of them signed the famous manifesto. From then on solitude surrounded the great physicist, and he found in Berlin the same odious and stupid militarism that had so disgusted him in his youth at school in Munich. He was not content with simply refusing to sign the manifesto of the ninety-three; he signed a counter-manifesto, a *Call to Europeans*, with Nicholai and Wilhelm Forster. He took part in the creation of a Berlin organization, the *Bund Neues Vaterland* — the Union of the New Fatherland — which set its goal in "fighting against chauvinism and preparing of public opinion for a peace which respects the honor of all fighting parties." It was through this action that Einstein learned of the position taken by Romain Rolland. Romain Rolland wrote to the scientist expressing his profound esteem for Einstein's courage, "I put at your disposal my feeble forces in case you think that I might be instrumental to you either by my situation or my association with German and foreign members of the academies of science." In September 1915 Einstein went to see Romain Rolland in Vevey. Rolland found him "very witty and lively; he can't keep himself from making us laugh with the most serious thoughts." And further he adds, "Anyone else might have suffered in feeling intellectually isolated, during this terrible year. Not him. He laughs."

On November 28, 1915 Einstein wrote to the physicist Arnold Sommerfeld: "During the course of this last month I have lived through the most stimulating and most trying period of my life, but in truth it was also the most fruitful." It is here, it seems to me, that we can grasp the man in all of his ingenuous complexity. Right in the middle of the war he wrote his major work *The Fundamentals of the General Theory of Relativity* which appeared in 1916 in the *Annals of Physics*. There was a whole side of Einstein which was entirely detached from what was happening at any time. He lived in another world, and nothing could prevent him from coming back to it each time he was called there. But he was also filled with a sense of duty towards humanity. No doubt he drew on his reading of Kant, whom he held in profound veneration; this also certainly came from his Jewish background, since there is no people more humane than the Jews, and it is for this same humanity that they have so often been persecuted. Einstein once wrote: "It was upon my arrival in Germany fifteen years ago that I discovered that I am Jewish and I owe this discovery more to non-Jews than to Jews." We can easily enough guess what such a sentence alludes to. For Einstein at this point all other considerations gave way to his duty towards humanity.

We now hold the key to this dialectic of detachment and involvement which was characteristic of him. Nothing was able to corrupt his sense of equity. One might truly say that Einstein was above human passions. Not that he was incapable of tenderness and affection toward his friends and family, much to the contrary; he suffered deeply over the illness of his second son Edouard, the death of Ilsa — Elsa's oldest daughter — and, above all, the death of Elsa herself. But he didn't allow these emotions to disturb the workings of his mind for long. What was totally foreign to him was the arbitrary pretenses which have made men of all time believe that they were capable of adding an inch to their own stature. Undoubtedly he was not far from understanding the essential causes of the violence and injustice in human history. When he yielded to these forces, it meant that he wasn't able to do otherwise, and he did so in the manner of a reasonable person who occasionally gives in to the fantasies of a child. In this case, however, the roles were reversed, because it was Einstein who seemed to behave himself as a child. Until his death he retained childlike qualities of freshness, curiosity, and a wonderful talent of surprise and spontaneity. It was Elsa who acted as an adult by his side. She patiently made him understand what was happening in a world which was different from his; when there were no other means she appealed to his heart, rarely in vain, because he never wanted to cause pain. But, for all this he had his own standards, which he had precisely defined once and for all. If these criteria seem strange to us now, it is because we are used to respecting arbitrary and quite often dangerous standards without really examining them ourselves. There is some childlike innocence in one of Einstein's most profound visions, as he asked of all things and, particularly of the human race itself, to justify itself.

Such was the man when probably the greatest fame ever to be experienced fell upon him. In 1917 he had published *Cosmological Remarks on the General Theory of Relativity*. "Modern cosmology was born in that year, 1917," his collaborator Infeld later wrote. What remained was to find the experimental proof of Einstein's ideas. This was the object of two important expeditions, organized in February 1919, to observe a total eclipse of the sun at Sobral, in northern Brazil, and on the island of Principe in the gulf of Guinea. They both demonstrated that Einstein's calculations were correct and that consequently it was necessary to renounce the construction of the world as it had been explained since Newton's time. One would imagine that Einstein was overjoyed at the news. But here is what Antonina Vallentin tells us, according to Elsa Einstein's memory, "He . . . looked [at the photographs] with a surprise that changed into joy, lighting up his face. 'It's marvelous, it's perfectly marvelous.' We thought he was all excited about his triumph. When the importance of the theory's confirmation was explained to Mrs. Einstein she timidly ventured, 'You must be happy about this, Albert!' And Einstein, his eyes still riveted to the photographs, said, 'I'm delighted.' But it was the quality of the pictures that he was speaking of because he immediately added, 'I would never have imagined that photography would come to such perfection.' '' His son-in-law, Dima, reports the same scene a little differently: One of Einstein's colleagues from Berlin University happened to be there when the photographs were delivered. He said to him "You must be happy. You are holding the proof of the accuracy of your theory in your hands." "Proof? . . . Proof?" Einstein repeated with the surprised questioning look that always gave one the impression that he was only a visitor on Earth. "Proof? They're the ones who needed proof. As far as I am concerned, I wasn't looking for it."

It was nevertheless the experimental proof that revealed Einstein to the world. In early November, 1919, these results were announced during a solemn meeting of the Royal Society of London. The president of the society spoke below a large portrait of Newton, saying, "It isn't a question here of the discovery of an isolated island, but of a whole continent of new scientific ideas. It is the greatest discovery concerning gravity since Newton announced his principles." This man, yesterday almost unknown, this German or Swiss Jew who came from a country with which England had just signed a peace treaty, was here proclaimed before the entire world as Newton's equal. That day there was as much glory for the English scientists as for Einstein himself.

Einstein became a legendary figure. Everybody knew his name, crowds thronged around him, and yet very few were actually able to understand the true nature of the revolution he had caused in science. The great physicist who presided over the meeting of the Royal Society declared "I must admit that up to the present moment no one has been able to tell me in simple words what Einstein's theory actually is." But the instinct of the masses is not always wrong. Einstein himself was the first one not to understand the immense fame which suddenly seized him. He was not however unconscious of the decisive progress he had just accomplished for the sake of human thought which had since milleniums tried to understand and explain the universe. When he said, for example: "It was an individual who discovered the cultivation of nutritious plants, it was an individual who discovered the steam engine," he spoke from experience. He, alone, had made such a discovery. Certainly he had men around him who had helped him, particularly mathematicians who patiently verified his calculations; but the essence of the research belonged to him alone. At times he felt as if he would never know if he would ever achieve his goal. One day he said to Alexander Moszkowski: "I would spend weeks in a state of complete confusion; and it was only with great difficulty that I overcame the stupor provoked by my first encounter with such questions." His son-in-law Marianogg reports the following conversation:

" 'Albert how is it that you came to make your discovery?'

" 'In a vision,' he answered me.'

"He told me that one day he had gone to bed in a state of discouragement so profound that no argument could put it to an end.

" 'When one reaches despair, nothing can help anymore, neither hours of work nor past success, nothing. All self-confidence disappears. It's over, I told myself, everything is useless. I haven't obtained any results . . . And that's when the thing came about.'

"With infinite precision, the universe and its secret unity of measure, structure, distance, time and space, such a monumental puzzle, was slowly reconstructed in Einstein's mind. And suddenly, as if printed by a giant printer, the immense map of the universe clearly unfolded itself in front of him in a dazzling vision. That is when he came to a sense of peace . . ."

Einstein at that point, was not unaware of the immense value of his solitary venture, nor of the heroism involved. It had made him physically ill several times. But he also thought that in acting in such a way he was only doing his duty. He was not responsible for his genius, he was only responsible for the use he made of it. The honors that over-whelmed him, the rewards that were pouring in probably did not seem to him unjustified, but he was profoundly indiffer-ent to them. I believe that the masses even sensed this in him, and Einstein only appeared greater because of his indif-ference, and moreover this indifference was never contemp-tuous. He even wished that his ideas could be made accessi-ble to everyone. He said "Legend pretends that science is only for men of science, but as it is a part of truth it must exist for everyone." In 1948, in the foreword to a book by Lincoln Barnett entitled *Einstein and the Universe*, he wrote, "It is of the greatest importance that the public at large has the opportunity of becoming aware — clearly and intelligently — of the efforts and results of scientific research* It isn't enough that a handful of specialists in each field attack a problem, solve it and apply it. To reduce and limit the body of knowledge to a small group annihilates the philosophic spirit of a people and leads to the most serious spiritual poverty!"

We must now give up following Einstein step by step. With fame began a period of widespread travel for him, but also a period during which he was to be confronted with the most painful and anguishing human problems. He learned, as we have seen, that he was Jewish; but it was not because of his background that he attached himself to Weizmann's Zionism. It was because Jews are a persecuted people, and it seemed just to him that they should find a national homeland in Palestine which the Balfour Declaration had promised them. He would have done the same for any other people

---

*In Chapter V, "Einstein, the Scientist," opens the present perspec-tive in physics for us.

who found themselves in the same situation. He was not ignorant of the fact that he compromised his friends and family with his militant Zionism. In March 1920 he saw with intense emotion the Kapp *coup d'état* fail in front of a general strike. He then renounced his Swiss citizenship and took back his German nationality, thus granting to the Wermar Republic what he had refused Wilhelm II's Reich. A little later he undertook a propaganda tour in America for the Jewish National Fund. He was astonished by the measure of his fame there. While he was travelling, no less celebrated, in the Far-East, he received the Nobel Prize for Physics. Finally, in 1922, he decided to go to Paris, where he found some of his best friends: Marie Curie, whom he had already known for a long time, Paul Painlevé and especially Paul Langevin, one of the men who was probably closest to his heart and mind.

He had hardly been back in Berlin when, on June 24, 1922, Walther Rathenau was assassinated by fanatics of the extreme right. Einstein himself had already been threatened, although he paid no attention to it. It was his wife who was subjected to keen anxiety and who persuaded him to accept an invitation from the University of Leyden (in Holland), where he spent three months. He became, at the time, an intimate friend of the Belgian royal couple Albert and Elisabeth. He said of the King, "He truly takes the trouble to understand." Einstein played music with the queen. This is how Antonina Vallentin describes one of their encounters: "When the queen asked him to come to Laeken, her summer residence, for the first time, she waited for him a long time. The chauffeur who had been sent to the train returned, saying that he hadn't seen anyone. Einstein was always precisely on time. The queen began to get alarmed. One of the ladies of the court was sent out to the park to watch for his arrival. Having waited for quite a time, she saw a man emerge on the path. He was covered with dust, his hair was waving as he walked. He was swinging a violin in his hand, and was gaily whistling. 'How was I supposed to know that you were going to send a car to the station?' Einstein replied in answer to the queen's questions. Later the chauffeur explained 'I didn't see anyone getting out of the first-class car. I couldn't imagine that one of Her Majesty's guests would be traveling in third!''

His adventures at the Commission for Intellectual Cooperation instituted by the League of Nations (which had admitted Einstein, although he was a German, because of his exceptional merit,) are narrated in Chapter VIII.

Einstein was always in the middle of it all; but in all his battles he never gave up the independence of his judgment. Of Lenin, for example, he said, ''I respect in Lenin the man who has completely sacrificed himself and who has devoted all his energy to the establishment of social justice. I don't consider his methods practical, but one thing is certain; men of his caliber are the guardians and restorers of human conscience.'' However he never responded to the invitations that he received from the Soviet Union. ''I never accepted their invitations,'' he said, ''because I am afraid that they would use my visit for political ends.''

We also remember his friendship with Charlie Chaplin, with Bernard Shaw, his conversations with Tagore . . .

But Hitler's sinister star was already rising over Germany. In 1929, Einstein was celebrating his fiftieth birthday. To honor him on this occasion the city of Berlin decided to offer him property on the shore of one of the lakes around Berlin which make the Brandenburg beautiful. They knew that the scientist loved sailing. Unfortunately, the city of Berlin did not own the house that they had wanted to offer, and they settled on another piece of ground located in a park; they discovered, however, that it was forbidden to build there. Finally Einstein found a place himself, one that was suitable for him, on the relatively high hill of Caputh, close to an attractive lake. But the municipal council would never vote the sum necessary to buy it. It was Anti-Semitism which was already creating the obstacles. Einstein bought the land with his own means and had a home built according to his taste. He was not, however, going to be able to enjoy it for long, because the Hitler storm continued to swell. But for once lacking his usual clairvoyance, Einstein refused to acknowledge it; he believed that certain things were impossible in Germany.

Einstein learned of Hitler's rise to power on a boat which was bringing him back from America to Europe. As soon as he disembarked he made this statement: "As long as I can do it, I will only live in a country where political freedom, tolerance and equality before the law reigns for all citizens. By political freedom I mean the freedom of power to express convictions verbally or in writing, and by tolerance, respect for all of an individual's convictions. "Presently these conditions are not fulfilled in Germany. People who have earned international recognition are being prosecuted here, and among them are some very eminent artists. As any individual, any social organization can become psychologically ill, especially in times when existence becomes hard. Generally nations survive such illnesses. I hope that Germany will soon recover her health and that in the future men like Kant and Goethe will not only be honored from time to time, but that the principles they taught will assert themselves in public life and in the conscience of all."* At the same time, Einstein sent his resignation to the Prussian Academy. They responded by accusing Einstein of taking part in a campaign to discredit Germany. Even the German Jews, who did not yet suspect what lay ahead of them, accused Einstein of

*In Chapter VI, "From Pacifism to the Bomb" Pierre-Henri Simon analyzes from a historical point of view the different aspects of the scientist's humanity.

being responsible, with his rigid attitude, for the misfortunes that they were experiencing. Anatole de Monzie, then the French Minister of Public Instruction, generously proposed that Einstein be offered a chair at the Collège de France, which Andler's death had just left vacant. Einstein accepted, but the Collège de France refused to change Andler's literary chair to a scientific chair and the Finance Commission didn't want to create a new chair. Thus, Einstein was never to become a professor at the Collège de France.

While he was waiting for something better, Einstein took up temporary residence on the Flemish coast, in a small resort town, Le Coq, thanks to the friendship of the Belgian sovereigns. But first he went to the German consulate in Brussels. "Never, in the course of all the years that I lived with him, have I seen Albert so upset," Elsa said. He calmly placed his German passport on the consulate's desk and asked which forms he had to fill out in order to renounce his citizenship. A little later the Nazis published a letter from the scientist in which he declared that if conflict were to break out between Germany and Belgium he would unhesitatingly offer his services to Belgium. One wonders about such an attitude in a pacifist as resolute as Einstein, but it is important to recall here what Dr. Millikan said of him: "The most extraordinary element of Einstein's greatness is his humility, the good will with which he is ready to change today what he said yesterday." Once when someone asked him how he had come to formulate the Theory of Relativity, he replied "By refusing to accept an axiom." [An axiom as we know, is a proposition or a principle that is universally accepted.]

At Le Coq, Einstein divided his time between his scientific work, helping the growing number of refugees, and a propaganda tour of England culminating in a meeting at the Albert Hall where Einstein, in the presence of some of England's most important personalities, condemned National Socialism before an agitated crowd, a crowd divided between enthusiasm and indignation. It was, according to all the witnesses, an unforgettable event. The great scientist addressed himself against Hitler in the manner of one of the ancient prophets of his people, crying out in the name of truth and justice. From then on, this was to be a fight to the finish between these two men, as between the forces of Good and Evil. The English Parliament's official reception of the great scientist certainly was not a negligible episode in the struggle against Hitler's Nazism.

Einstein became a citizen of the world. He could not stay long in Belgium for many reasons, and first of all because his life, in spite of the precautions taken, was not safe there. He accepted the offer that Princeton University's Institute for Advanced Study made to him. He spent the last twenty years of his life there in a studious and wonderfully preserved solitude, forty miles from New York. The Einsteins bought a house on Mercer Street, and Elsa did her best to furnish it with what they had been able to get from Berlin.

Another personal drama was going to upset Einstein's peaceful life in Princeton: one of Elsa's two daughters, Ilsa, died in Paris while her parents were in the United States. Elsa was never able to console herself over this loss. Barely had she prepared the house on Mercer Street when she fell ill herself; she died in 1936. From then on Einstein lived alone, with no companions other than his faithful secretary, his collaborators and occasionally his daughter Margot. He said ''I live in the solitude that is painful in youth and delicious in old age.'' For Einstein, these were great, productive years. He was putting the finishing touches on his unified field theory.

Einstein was happy in the United States. Later, after America entered the war, he was troubled to see the development of a militarism which unhappily reminded him of Germany under Wilhelm II. But the principal object in his life, aside from his scientific work, was the struggle against

Hitler. He vigorously aided victims of Nazism, and he wrote, "It is embarrassing to be the object of so much respect and so much affection. The arrows of hate have also been flung at me, but they have never touched me because in a way they belonged to another world, with which I have absolutely no connections." Whatever he said about solitude, we must recognize that, in his last years, the gap continued to deepen around him. It was not because of his enemies, whose blows he did not feel, but because of his fellow scientists, who no longer followed the more and more deserted path that he chose to tread. Infeld, for example, reports "When I discussed this problem with Einstein himself he told me 'Man has little luck.' " In the autumn of 1944 Einstein wrote to his friend Sommerfeld, "We have come to stand at opposite poles regarding our scientific ideas and what we expect from science. You, you believe in the good Lord who plays dice, and I believe in perfect laws, in a world of things existing as real objects, which I try to conceive in a fiercely speculative manner."*

But there was another drama in Einstein's life, infinitely closer to all of us, that of his responsibility in the development of the atomic bomb. (See Chapter VI.)

"In fact," Einstein later said to Antonina Vallentin, "I simply served as the mail box. They brought me a letter which had already been drawn up, and all I had to do was to sign it."

"Just the same, you pressed the button."

"Yes, I pressed the button."

Later he repeated many times, "If I had known for sure that the Nazi's wouldn't succeed in making the bomb before the Allies, I would have abstained from participating in whatever happened."

*In Chapter VII, "The Philosopher-Scientist," Francois Russo studies the philosophical importance of Einstein's methods and theories.

We know what followed. The last ten years of Einstein's life were devoted, on one hand, to pursuing his work on the unified field theory, and, on the other, to the struggle to allow the secret of the bomb to be communicated to the Soviets, and for the establishment of a world government. "The war is won, but not peace," he wrote. And, to Antonina Vallentin, "These last years have produced an evil worse than anything that the most inveterate pessimists could have imagined. But the strangest fact is that we have throughout our actions taken such pains to gain a sense of justice and equity, whereas it would have been far better if the consciousness that we have taken of the very roots of evil had taught us a lesson." "Perhaps," he also added, "the human experience was only a mistake." And again, "The real problem lies in the hearts of men." In December 1946 Einstein learned of the death of his friend Paul Langevin and he wrote: "The news of Paul Langevin's death affects me more painfully than most of the events of these distressing years, so many disillusions . . . There are so few men in a generation who manage to bring together a clear understanding of the nature of things, an intense emotion for all truly humanitarian needs and a capacity for militant action. When such a man goes, he leaves a void which seems unbearable to those who survive him."

During her last visit to Princeton, Antonina Vallentin poignantly felt this void around Einstein, this melancholy which no longer gave way to his customary laughter. She immediately perceived the mortal anguish which had taken hold of this great soul and finally killed it."*

In saying good-bye to his friend, he said to her, as if to excuse himself for being more silent than usual, for signing even fewer manifestos, "At the right moment, you know,

*In Chapter VII, Hilaire Cuny remembers Einstein "Such as We Knew Him" thanks to the most outstanding testimony of those who were close to him.

my voice will carry more weight. I am waiting for that moment. Then I will scream with all the strength that I have left in me.'' I remember Antonina Vallentin repeating Einstein's words to me just before his death. In fact, Einstein died without having spoken, of an inflammation of the biliary vesicle. Thomas Mann said, ''Can we doubt that the sorrow caused in him by the world's deplorable evolution and the atrocious threat that his science had innocently lent its counsel to had contributed to his body's illness, to the final attack, and abbreviated his life?'' He once said, ''I bother people very much, simply because I am there.''

What finally happened to the life of this genius, who more than anyone else, enlarged the field of human knowledge and who never shied away from his simple human duties?* Was it wasted? I think not. Even if Einstein had not been such an incredible genius, we would still have to recognize in him the man who revered justice, one of those whose presence is enough to save the cursed cities from a shower of fire. He has been dead for more than ten years [Ed. in this text] but his example survives, and gives us the right to hope that God, who he said is shrewd but not vindictive, will create as many fair people as are necessary to allow humanity, finally reconciled with itself, to progress peacefully in the joy of knowledge.

All great success is obtained through great pain. Isolated and stricken with doubt and grief in his Princeton home, Einstein remains an exemplary image of the human condition. Having taken it upon himself, he was the instrument of a progress which we cannot yet measure even in a moral context.

---

*Louis Armand concludes with an homage to the ''Grandeur of Einstein'' in Chapter IX.

CHAPTER TWO

Einstein and Physics

by LOUIS DE BROGLIE *of the Académie Française*
Life Secretary of the Academy of Science
Nobel Prize in Physics

To every cultivated man, whether or not he is devoted to the study of some branch of science, the name Albert Einstein exemplifies human inspiration and intelligence. Upsetting the most traditional ideas in Physics, Einstein succeeded in establishing the relativity of the notions of space and time, the inertia of energy and a purely geometric interpretation of the forces of gravity. There lies an impressive achievement, comparable to the greatest works in the history of science, those of Isaac Newton, for example; this accomplishment alone is enough to assure its author of eternal renown. But, as great as this work is, it should not completely overshadow Einstein's other decisive contributions to contemporary Physics. Even if we leave aside the remarkable work that he accomplished in Brownian motion, statistical thermodynamics, and fluctuation, we cannot fail to recognize the immense importance of the research he devoted to the birth of the quantum theory and, in particular, his conception of "quantum light", optically re-introducing the corpuscular image, which had hindered physicists search for a kind of

synthesis of Fresnel's wave theory of light and the old particle theory. Throughout this work, Einstein found himself at
the origin of a movement of ideas which, twenty years later,
under the names of wave mechanics and quantum
mechanics, came to throw such a troubled light on all the
phenomena of the atomic scale.

Albert Einstein wrote numerous treatises, especially in
his youth, but almost all of these reports are short; he only
wrote a few concise summaries. Generally, he has left others
with the task of representing in completed form the theories
which his powerful thought had created. However, while all
these articles are brief, there are none that do not contain
either admirable new ideas destined to revolutionize science
or fine and profound comments affecting the most hidden
aspects of the problem which are discussed, opening almost
unlimited perspectives in few words. Einstein's work is
above all a "work of quality" from which all compilation and
detailed development are excluded. We can compare his
treatises to fireworks, which illuminate a vast, shadowy
territory with a sudden but powerful light.

Throughout the researches that he undertook, Einstein
always knew — and here lies the mark of his genius — how to
master all questions that he asked himself and how to vis-
ualize them in a context which went beyond the knowledge
of all of his predecessors. Thus, in the formulas of the
Lorentz Transformation, he did not, as others had before
him, see a simple mathematical device, but rather, the very
expression of the physical relationship between space and
time. Thus, again, in the laws governing the photo-electric
effect, unanticipated and inexplicable by classic ideas, he
perceived the necessity of somehow getting back to the
particle conception of light. We could find numerous examples, all proving to us the inspired originality of a mind which
knew how to perceive at first glance, new and simple facts
which unveiled the true meaning and suddenly shed light

where darkness had reigned, through a maze of complex and difficult questions.

This does not diminish the merit of other great discoverers, it only points out how their finds came in their own time, prepared in a way by all of the previous work which had been accomplished. The fruit was ripe, but until then no one perceived it nor knew how to pick it.

In 1905, Albert Einstein, with marvelous intuition, set forth the principle of relativity and pointed out its significance and scope. For the previous twenty years, scientists had been having difficulties with older theories. They had not, however, succeeded in discovering the source of their problems. These old theories, in effect, allowed for the existence of ether, that is to say of a tenuous substance filling up all of space and serving, we might say, to materialize the classic notion of absolute space. This substance, supporting all light and electrical phenomena, remained very mysterious. Even after half a century of research, Fresnel's followers could not reasonably explain ether's physical properties, and in the basically abstract theories of the electro-magnetic field developed notably by Maxwell, Hertz and Lorentz, this substance played hardly more than a secondary role. Even reduced to this modest role, the substance was still troublesome, for, although its existence led to predictions about phenomena of relative motion in relation to ether, these phenomena were not actually happening. Interferential measure afforded greater accuracy, thereby allowing physicists like Michelson to confirm the non-existence of effects of the Earth's motion in relation to ether on optical phenomena, thus discarding previously held theories. The theorists, moved by this discrepancy between predicted theories and observation, had examined the question from all sides, submitting the electromagnetic theory to all kinds of critical studies and revisions. H.A. Lorentz, the great specialist in these matters, noticed an important fact: examining the manner in which Maxwell's equations were transformed in passing from one reference system to another, in a rectilinear and uniform motion in regard to the first, he demonstrated that these equations remained unchanged when certain variables were linked to the initial variables by particular linear relationships. This constitutes what, since then, has been called the "Lorentz Transformation." Lorentz considered them only as imaginary variables, facilitating certain calculations. Nevertheless, advancing much closer to the real solution of the problem, he had defined, with the aid of the variable 't', a *local time* (one specific point in time) while Fitzgerald, interpreting Lorentz' formulas in his own way, attributed the failure in Michelson's experiments to a flattening, a longitudinal contraction that all solid bodies undergo in motion. The Lorentz Transformation, local time, and Fitzgerald's contraction were all expedients allowing the discovery of certain aspects of the properties of the electromagnetic field without being able to clearly explain their deeper significance. Then came Albert Einstein.

With great boldness he approached this formidable problem, which had already been the object of so much research, placing himself resolutely at a new point of view. For him, the formulas of the Lorentz Transformation weren't simple mathematical concepts defining a convenient change of variables used in the study of electromagnetic equations; they were the expression of the relation which exists "physically" between the co-ordinates of space and time for two Galilean observers. It was a daring hypothesis, before which Lorentz' shrewd mind had retreated. It effectively brought about the abandon of the traditional notions which had been accepted since the time of Newton, concerning the absolute nature of space and time. It established an unforeseen relationship between these two elements of the framework which orders all of our perceptions — a relationship completely contrary to our initial intuitive response to observable data.

It was due to Albert Einstein's extraordinary brilliance that he was able to succeed in establishing his framework for space and time by the means of a fine and profound analysis of the physicists' system of measure. He thus demonstrated that the co-ordinates of space and time for varying Galilean observers are linked to each other by Lorentz' formulas, and proved that the non-existence of signals propagating themselves with infinite speed makes it impossible to verify the simultaneous occurrence of two distant events. He analyzed the way in which observers in the same Galilean system nevertheless manage, by synchronizing their clocks with an exchange of signals, to mark a simultaneity in their reference system. However, this simultaneity would only be valid for them, and the events which thus appeared simultaneous to them would not appear so to observers moving in relation to them. In this reasoning the essential fact is that no signal can be diffused at a greater speed than that of light in a vacuum.

As soon as Albert Einstein had laid the foundation for the Theory of Relativity, innumerable interesting consequences proceeded from these strange new ideas. The Lorentz-Fitzgerald contraction, the apparent slowing down of clocks in motion, the variation of mass with speed in the motion of rapid particles, new formulas containing supplementary terms for the aberration, and the Doppler effect, new formulas for the composition of speed allowing the direct discovery, as a simple consequence of relativist kinematics, of Fresnel's famous formula — verified by Fizeau — yielding the flow of light waves through refracted bodies in motion — such are the principal consequences of Einstein's conceptions. And these are not simply unproven theories. We cannot overemphasize the fact that the special Theory of Relativity today rests on innumerable verified experiments, for now we know how to track particles moving at speeds close to that of light in a vacuum, a process which must take into account the corrections introduced by the Theory of Relativity.

Surely, some of the consequences of the Theory of Relativity had been noticed by various theorists and notably by H.A. Lorentz and Henri Poincaré but these observations had been done independently from one another. However as remarkable as their results were, only Einstein's vigorous synthesis made them appear in their true light, as flowing out of the same fundamental principle.

If the special Theory of Relativity has thus been directly verified by experiment, it has also proved its worth in serving as a point of departure for fruitful new theories. It also intervenes in the theory of photons (quanta of light) and in that of the Compton Effect. It is verified in the study of the photoelectric effect and in that of the diffraction of electrons in dealing with particles of very great speed where variation of the mass with the speed is perceptible. The introduction of relativist dynamics in Bohr's atomic theory permitted Sommerfeld to obtain for the first time, a theory of the complex structure of spectral rays which, in its time, constituted considerable progress.

We cannot forget the role that relativist ideas have played in the development of wave mechanics. Finally Dirac's electromagnetic theory allowed a relativist theory to be obtained on spinning particles, and demonstrated that a strong and rather hidden link does exist between relativist ideas and the notion of spinning.

Today we cannot make an analysis, even a very summary one, of the special Theory of Relativity without mentioning the inertia of energy. In relativist dynamics, the expression of the energy of a material point demonstrates that in each Galilean reference system, energy is equal to the square of the speed of light in a vacuum times the mass which the material point discussed possesses, by virtue of its motion in this reference system. Therefore, from this statement, Albert Einstein concluded that all mass necessarily corresponds to an energy equal to the product of this mass times the square of the speed of light. He demonstrated how we can verify this idea in particular cases through brilliant examples. Thus, the two principles of conservation of mass and conservation of energy, until then considered as absolutely distinct, now came to be associated with each other in certain ways. Since radiation carries energy, it follows that a body which radiates loses mass and a body which absorbs radiant energy acquires mass. Moreover, these new ideas were in accord with the existence of radiant energy movement which had been uncovered by the work of Henri Poincaré and Max Abraham.

One of the most important consequences of this principle of the inertia of energy is that the least fragment of matter, by the fact of its mass, contains an enormous quantity of energy. Matter has since been seen as an immense reserve of energy congealed, so to speak, in the form of mass. From then on, the thought emerged that one day, man might succeed in freeing and using a part of this hidden treasure. We now know, exactly forty years after Einstein's initial work in relativity, just how shocking and frightening was the materialization of that very idea.

The Theory of Relativity is an impressive but incomplete monument. In effect, it only involves the description of phenomena in Galilean reference systems, that is to say in reference systems which are in rectilinear and uniform motion in regard to fixed stars. On the one hand, it only concerns the changes of variables corresponding to rectilinear and uniform relative motion, and on the other hand it allows a kind of primacy to reference systems lined to the whole system of fixed stars. It was necessary to break away from these restrictions in constructing a more general theory extending the principle of relativity to include any accelerated motion and linking the character of acceleration, apparently absolute, to the existence of all stellar masses. From the beginning of his work, Albert Einstein was very conscious of the necessity for such a generalization, and succeeded little by little in finding the much sought-after solution. In this research he was guided by the remarks of certain predecessors, such as Mach, and by his great knowledge of tensorial calculus and absolute differential calculus which had already been of some use in the Theory of Relativity. But here again it was the inspired originality of his mind that permitted him to reach the goal which was definitively achieved in 1916.

Relying on the Riemannian theory of curved space, the General Theory of Relativity developed, utilizing all the resources of tensorial calculus, an interpretation of the phenomena of gravity the grandeur and elegance of which cannot be disputed. It remains one of the most beautiful moments in mathematical Physics of the twentieth century.

The General Theory of Relativity tends to give a geometric interpretation of the notion of "force". It certainly accomplishes its end insofar as the forces of gravitation are concerned. However, its goal would have been entirely achieved, then, if it had also succeeded in interpreting electromagnetic forces, because in this era when the existence of nuclear forces were still unknown, one could have thought that all the forces existing in nature were either gravitational or electromagnetic. But electromagnetic forces are proportional to the charge of the body on which they act and not on its mass. The result is that the trajectory of an electrified material point in an electromagnetic field depends on the relation of its charge to its mass and varies according to the nature of the material point. There is a fundamental difference here between the gravitational field and the electromagnetic field, which does not permit the geometric interpretation that works for the former to be extended to the latter. For thirty years, innumerable attempts have been made to complete the Theory of General Relativity on this point and to transform it into a "unified theory" capable of interpreting the existence of gravitational forces and electromagnetic forces at the same time. Naturally, Einstein also worked on possible solutions to this problem and published numerous treatises on the new forms of this unifying theory, some alone, others with collaborators. Despite their indisputable interest, these theories did not, to our knowledge, result in a decisive success, rather they formed landmarks along a path which still has to be cleared. Moreover, the nature of the electromagnetic field is so intimately connected to the existence of quantum phenomena that any non-quantum unifying theory is then logically incomplete. These are problems of a formidable complexity the solution of which is still "in the hands of the gods".

Albert Einstein's work relative to fluctuation, Brownian motion and statistical thermodynamics probably has a lesser overall importance than his brilliant research on the Theory of Relativity. However, it was sufficient to add to his renown as a great Physicist. Accomplished during the period 1905-1912, and developed parallel to Smoluchovski's remarkable theoretical work on the same subject, it had its worth because, at that time, people were seeking everywhere direct or indirect proof of the existence of molecules. A great many experimenters, in the forefront of which were Jean Perrin and The Svedberg, had then, through the observation of equilibrium in emulsions, Brownian motion, fluctuations of density, critical opalescence, etc. . . . furnished the decisive proof needed for the existence of molecules. All of this work had been guided and illuminated by Einstein's calculations. And the concepts or methods which Einstein, with his usual seriousness, had introduced in the course of his theoretical research also projected a new light on certain aspects of the statistical interpretation of thermodynamics.

To be brief, I am obliged to pass rapidly over this nevertheless important part of Albert Einstein's work. I must, on the other hand, discuss the major contributions that he made in the development of quantum theory. We should not forget that it was in particular for this work on the photo-electric effect that he was awarded the Nobel Prize for Physics in 1921.

When Einstein undertook his first researches, Planck, in his memorable work, had just introduced the surprising quantum hypothesis. He had demonstrated that it permitted the discovery of experimental laws concerning the spectral distribution of rays of thermal equilibrium, which the classic theories had not succeeded in explaining. Planck had admitted a disturbing supposition completely disagreeing with the most inveterate concepts of ancient physics — that electronic oscillators which are responsible inside matter for the emission and absorption of rays, can only emit radiant energy in quanta, of a value proportional to the emitted frequency. Thus, this led to the introduction of the famous Planck's constant, as a proportional factor, the importance of which, in relation to phenomena of atomic scale, continues to be confirmed more and more as time goes by. Planck thus obtained the correct law of black radiation and, comparing his formula with results coming from experiments, he extracted the value of the constant h. Moreover, the introduction of the quantum hypothesis proved to be necessary in order to obtain a correct representation of the properties of the black radiation. The work of Lord Rayleigh, Jeans, Planck himself and, a little earlier, Henri Poincaré, proved that the former concepts led unavoidably to inaccurate laws and that the introduction of the element of discontinuity represented by quantum of action was inevitable.

The young Einstein abandoned himself to profound reflection on this difficult subject and in 1905, at the age of twenty-six, right when he laid the foundations of the Theory of Relativity, he proposed to place himself at the most radical point of view, admitting the hypothesis of a granular structure of radiation, and he extracted from that an interpretation of the mysterious laws of photo-electric effects. Thus, of the two great theories that today reign over the entire world of contemporary Physics — those of relativity and quantum — Einstein founded one and achieved major progress in the other in the same year and with the inspired energy of an exceptional mind.

Einstein's concepts were immediately strongly opposed. The great masters of science, such as Lorentz and Planck, had no difficulty in demonstrating that a particle theory of light could not explain the phenomena of diffraction and coherence of wave patterns, for which the wave theory offered a simple interpretation. Einstein did not deny these difficulties but he asserted the necessity of introducing an element of discontinuity into light waves, supporting his assertions with penetrating commentary. He was inclined towards a "mixed theory" which admitted the existence of particles of radiant energy but which linked their motion and their localization to the propagation of a homogeneous wave of the Maxwell-Fresnel type. Later, at the beginning of the development of wave mechanics, I attempted to develop an analaguous idea in order to interpret the general relation between the particles and their associated waves. These attempts failed and it was necessary to come to a very different interpretation, one connected to Heisenberg's relationships of uncertainty. But it is certain that Einstein's ideas on the constitution of light have played a decisive role in the evolution of quantum theory and the breakthrough of wave mechanics.

Nevertheless, quantum theory was making enormous progress elsewhere. In 1913, Bohr published his quantified theory of the atom which had immense repercussions in the whole field of Physics. In 1916, Sommerfeld perfected Bohr's theory, introducing the corrections of relativity and realizing, at least partially, the fine structures observed in the spectrums. Einstein followed all this work with great interest. In one of his treatises, he precisely noted the method of quantification that Sommerfeld employed and, when Bohr announced his "principle of correspondence", he published his celebrated work in which, studying thermodynamic equilibrium between Planck's formula and Bohr's frequency laws and, in agreement with the principle of correspondence, he expressed the probability of quantified transitions that can be sustained by an atom plunged into surrounding radiation. Once again he brought a valuable contribution to the development of quantum theory.

When, in 1924, I stated the ideas which lie at the base of wave mechanics in my doctoral thesis, Einstein learned of them through an intermediary, Paul Langevin and, appreciating their value, in January 1925, he published a piece in the *Berlin Academy Review* in which, leaning on these new ideas and on the recent work of the Hindu Physicist Bose, he defined the statistics applicable to a group of particles indistinguishable from one another. These statistics, which are applicable to photons, to alpha particles and more generally to all complex particles containing an even number of elementary particles, today carry the name of "Bose-Einstein statistics". As we now know, electrons, protons, neutrons and complex particles formed by an odd number of elementary particles are placed under Pauli's principle of exclusion and their grouping obeys different statistics, those of Fermi-Dirac. By attracting attention to some new ideas of wave mechanics, Einstein's treatise certainly contributed a great deal to the development of this new branch of Physics.

The first half of the twentieth century was marked by the extraordinarily sudden expansion of Physics which remains one of the most brilliant chapters in the history of science. In these few years, human science raised two monuments which will continue to stand through the centuries: the Theory of Relativity and the quantum theory. The first was born entirely in the creative mind of Albert Einstein; the second, for which Planck had laid the first stones, owes to Einstein some of its most admirable developments.

We cannot contemplate a work that is at the same time so profound and so powerfully original without astonishment and admiration. It was accomplished in just a few years. The name of Albert Einstein will always be attached to two of the most magnificent achievements of which the human mind can be proud.

Author's Note: I have today again taken up the kinds of research mentioned and I am convinced that it is in this direction that we will find the true interpretation of the coexistence of waves and particles (note added in 1966).

CHAPTER THREE

Before Einstein

by THEO KAHAN
Professor, Paris Faculté des Sciences

At the dawn of philosophic thought the Greek mind discovered the scientific approach to nature; in order to give reason to the motion of the heavens and terrestrial phenomena. From the beginning, the Greek genius learned to mistrust the rhapsody of the senses, the feelings of terror and adoration created by religious feelings, and to reject the fantasies of the aberrant imagination which never stopped subjugating man. The ancient Greek thinkers understood that the spectacle that the universe offers us constitutes a world of appearances where it is important to give reason by means of the intellect. Modern science is thus indebted to them for the notion of natural law, for the mathematical explanation of phenomena — didn't Pythagoras proclaim that "all things are numbers?" — for the creation of Euclidian geometry and finally, last but not least, for the atomic theory. These incomparable discoveries were to stamp with their indelible seal all further scientific and philosophic conceptions in the last three centuries.

These three centuries have seen the birth, one after the other, of mechanics, electromagnetics, optics, thermodynamics, and the development of modern atomic theory. Our intention here is to quickly sketch a painting of the state of these sciences before the publication of Einstein's first work.

Modern dynamics — the science treating the motion of objects and the connections between their forces and the motion that these forces produce — is the eminent work of Galileo, Huxgens and, especially, Newton. It rests on two pillars, or theorems: (1) the force to which an object is subjected is equal to its mass times its acceleration, and (2) the mutual forces between the two masses are equal but of opposite signs — the principle of action and reaction. Here we should note that it is a question of "inert" mass, defined by the two former theorems, which is the measure of the inertia that an object opposes to the acceleration of its motion when something is affecting it: if two masses are put in motion through mutual acceleration, the accelerations will be inversely proportional to the masses.

The founding of mechanics is narrowly linked to the theory of gravity. The problem of gravity — just like that of atoms — has absorbed the human mind since time immemorial. Galileo, like Newton, demonstrated that all bodies undergo the same acceleration in a free fall; they also verified that a pendulum, which owes its motion to the forces of gravity, swings for a period of time which depends on its length and not at all on the nature of the object which is oscillating. The phenomena of gravity also calls to mind the notion of mass, which is the weight of the object. This notion has been named more massive mass by opposition to its less massive mass. One of the most striking facts to come out of the study of gravitation was the confirmation that this more massive mass is equal to the inert mass in each object.

We owe the majestic structure of celestial mechanics to Newton's genius. After having accumulated the results of experiments dealing with terrestrial gravitation, he generalized them in order to express universal attraction.

Using as a basis his law of attraction — two masses are attracted to each other in inverse proportion in relation to the squares of the distances separating them — Newton deduced Kepler's laws relative to planetary orbits, interpreting the irregularity in the moon's motion, and its effect on earthly tides. Is it necessary to emphasize the extraordinary stir that Newton's law created among his contemporaries, an interpretation that was so much more profound than the position taken before him, which held that the position of the planets was a direct manifestation of divine will. This discovery put an immediate end to the credibility of astrology. This was the debut of scientific power which, from then on, no other power would be able to defy with impunity.

Newtonian mechanics developed originally from certain fundamental concepts from which it is inseparable and which serve to support it; those of spatial and temporal spheres which are real and not qualitatively differentiated and which contain all objects. In this view space and time, the seat of all things and phenomena, are infinite, homogeneous and absolute. These classical mechanics are based on notions of mass and force, and the concept of immutable, absolute space and times unfurling uniformly in a homogeneous and absolute manner. Let's add that this space is provided with a Euclidian structure which further expresses its perpetual character. It is in this framework, thus defined, that all phenomena occur in a natural and predictable manner; nature is the seat of this system.

However, Newton's law of universal gravitation implies, in the mind of its author, action at a distance without an intermediary medium, the instantaneous transmittal of gravitation. If we could suddenly create a new mass, the effect of its appearance would immediately make itself felt throughout the universe. The idea of such an action at a distance, despite the major reservations that it encountered, triumphed under the influence of Newtonian discoveries. It

wound up invading other fields in physics. While the
mechanics of objects had always been defined by an action
which was gradually transmitted, the first theories of magnetic and electric phenomena were drafted on the idea of action
at a distance. It was only in the second half of the nineteenth
century that a radical change occurred in the problem of
action at a distance, following the work done by Faraday and
Maxwell, and especially after Hertz's discovery of electromagnetic waves,* waves which are propagated at very
high speeds but limited by light. Since then gravitational
action at a distance lost all credit, but it was necessary to wait
for the advent of relativity for this problem to be emptied of
its content.

The modern interpretation of electric and magnetic
phenomena is the work of Faraday and Maxwell. The study
of dielectric and diamagnetic properties of substances led the
first to think that electric and magnetic action, far from being
instantaneously transmitted from one object to another, find
themselves conveyed by the dielectric currents** which
separate them, this dielectric current being a king of seat for
an electric or magnetic "field."

Maxwell took on the task of elaborating, extending, and
deepening the physics and mathematics of this major idea of
field, seat and vehicle of interactions, and the associated
notion of the line of force. Completing the work done by
Ampere and Faraday, Maxwell introduced the idea of elec-

---

*Waves which are diffracted by obstacles and which interfere with
one another (like light waves).

** The dielectric and diamagnetic properties of an object are its characteristics regarding the electric current or the magnetic field. They are
two essential properties of each definite compound, as important for
its knowledge as its density or its specific heat.

tromagnetic radiation and established the system of equations governing electrodynamics which bears his name. This system of differential equations, of singular formal beauty, constitutes the basis of modern electromagnetic physics, along with the complements given by Hertz, Poynting, Lorentz and Poincaré. Maxwell's theory, despite its internally logical coherence and its numerous experimental proofs, encountered a stubborn resistance, like all truly new and productive ideas, from other physicists at the time of its publication, a resistance that only gave way with Hertz's discovery of electromagnetic waves.

Just as Newton had opened the era of the mathematical elaboration of mechanics, Maxwell's work was at the origin of an analytic development of his concepts. Thus Maxwell's theory assumed, with its definitive state, the character of an incomparable masterpiece, attaining the same level of perfection as celestial mechanics.

Let's also remark, before leaving the electromagnetic field, the phenomena called "photo-electric", which played such an important role in Albert Einstein's scientific career. In 1887 Hertz observed that ultraviolet light facilitates the passage of a spark through a gas; the following year Hallwachs demonstrated that this phenomenon is connected to the appearance of particles carrying electric charges in the gas. Here was the first indication of the influence of light on electricity, a kind of counterpart to Hertz's verification of the common nature of electromagnetic waves and light. In 1899 Lenard identified the carriers of charges as electrons and in 1902 announced an empirical law, at first very surprising, of the phenomena of the action of light on the appearance of these electrons: the energy of the electrons emitted by a metal under the effect of light depends on the frequency of the radiation employed in the bombardment, but is independent of the intensity of the light's vibrations; this intensity only determines the number of electrons in the unit of time. This phenomenon revealed itself as being absolutely irreconcilable with the wave theory of light.

Classical thermodynamics — which is concerned with the relations between heat, work and energy and used to be known as the mechanical theory of heat — is based on three principles. The first is the principle of the conservation of energy which holds that heat is a form of energy susceptible to being measured in mechanical terms. It expresses the equivalence between the two forms of energy and indicates the impossibility of perpetual motion in the first kind, that is the impossibility of obtaining work from nothing. The importance of this principle is such that it is further discussed.

The first to establish a connection between mechanical work and heat was uncontestably Sadi Carnot.* Later Robert Meyer also considered electrical and biological processes, even astrophysical ones — the origin of solar heat, terrestrial tides . . . : Parting from philosophical principles such as *ex nihilo nihil fit* and *nil fit ad nihilum*, he applied them to the ''force of falling'', to motion and to heat, and ended with the correct evaluation of a mechanical equivalent to heat.

If we stress Meyer's reasoning it is because here we are able to grasp the fundamental tendency of the human mind: the research into quantity or dimension which remain constant, invariable in the course of incessantly changing things. In fact, as the major task of physics is the discovery of general laws in nature, and as the simplest form of such laws consists in expressing the invariability of certain dimensions in physics, the search for such constants is not only justified because of its conformity to the demands of the human mind, it also represents an orientation of the highest importance in the entire evolution of science. We see the same tendency in

---

*The uncle of one of the presidents of the Third Republic in France, during the nineteenth century, assassinated by Caserio.

the work related to the discovery of the conservation of the quantity of electricity. Certainly only an experiment can decide if the dimension preserves itself with no variant. Just as the principle of the conservation of electricity is an empirical fact, that of the conservation of energy is also.

When, around 1860, the principle of the conservation of energy was universally admitted, it immediately became the keystone of all sciences. Enthusiasm stirred some philosophies, called "energism," which proposed to deduce all the laws in physics from this principle of energy. And yet the champions of these concepts misunderstood the irreducible character of the second principle of thermodynamics, in spite of Planck's pertinent objections and, more particularly, in spite of Boltzmann's criticism, based on atomistics and statistics. Finally, energerics, like so many erroneous doctrines, disappeared when its proponents died.

The second principle of thermodynamics lies in the impossibility of perpetual motion, called the "second kind" of motion, that is to say the impossibility of creating a periodic machine whose operation could accomplish anything other than the internal conversion of heat into mechanical work. If such an apparatus could exist, we could be able to make heat pass continually from a cold object into a warmer one without any compensation. Now this is impossible and the second principle of thermodynamics only confirms this impossibility.

The first principle, establishing the equivalence between heat and mechanical work, created a kind of function translating the state of an object. This is energy. The second principle also led to the appearance of a function, called "entropy", which translates the impossibility of realizing certain transformations. If we take a system comprised of a certain number of objects — molecules, atoms, etc. — which are able to affect each other, and if we isolate this system from all exterior influences, the entire energy would not vary during the course of all the events that would take place in the interior of this system. It is precisely the principle of invariance. On the contrary, entropy will only increase; only the phenomena that will increase this entropy can occur. More and more abstract notions are at that point being raised in physics.

Theoretically, after having defined these two notions of the independent states of energy and entropy, scientists should have been able to use analytical mathematics to describe the behavior of various objects from the thermic point of view. However one difficulty appeared in the beginning: one could only calculate these two dimensions in a system in relation to something else, to an initial state. It was necessary to choose this arbitrarily. We will see that, regarding energy, this indetermination was suppressed by Einstein's law of the equivalence of energy and mass; regarding entropy the problem was solved by the third principle of thermodynamics, Nernst's theory which states that the entropy of a chemically homogeneous object tends towards zero when the temperature of the object comes close to the absolute zero.

The scope of the laws which make up the structure of classical thermodynamics is defined by the fact that common, existing phenomena are irreversibly evolving, that is to say outside of any equilibrium, whereas the laws are only valid for ideal, reversible and infinitely slow operations. At that point, equations are transformed into inequalities. To calculate entropy, modern physics use statistical methods, which go beyond the limits of classical thermodynamics. (These methods will be discussed in the section devoted to atomism.) It is precisely in statistics that all the importance of entropy appears. In fact, classical thermodynamics could even do without the notion of entropy, because within its framework one can always, at least mentally, use a cycle of careful transformations which in each particular case allow for a new reasoning which, once generalized, leads to the concept of entropy. On the other hand, the idea of entropy is indispensable to the methods of statistical thermodynamics. It played a decisive role in the discovery of Planck's quantum law.

Atomic theory was first an elaborate philosophical concept, without recourse to experiment, created by Democrites and his school. Under its scientific aspect, it came to light at the beginning of the last century in Dalton's work. On one hand, Dalton postulated that all the atoms — elementary particles — of a chemical element, and all the molecules of a compound, possess identical properties. On the other he defined atomic weight as being the mass of an atom, taking an atom of hydrogen as the unit of measure. In fact, we encounter the first application of the notion of atoms and molecules in the kinetic theory of gas, where it is admitted that the pressure exerted by gas on the inner surface of a receptacle enclosing it is due to the incessant and disorderly bouncing of animated molecules at different speeds, which depend on the temperature of the gas. The relationship between the temperature and the distribution of speeds animating the diverse molecules at varied speeds is given by a law called the "Maxwell-Bolzmann law." Towards the middle of the last century a correct idea had already been delineated regarding the size and number of gaseous molecules; regarding the sizes, these molecules were found to have a diameter of 10^{-8} cm, and there were estimated to be approximately 10^{22} of them per cubic centimeter of gas under normal conditions of temperature and pressure.

All the reasoning in the kinetic theory of gas was based on the hypothesis of rigid gaseous molecules, very hard and spherically shaped, continually bouncing against each other. Little by little one got rid of these simplifying hypotheses, extending the theory to the internal motion of atoms making up the molecules, to their rotation and vibration, and thus one was able to successfully demonstrate that there is an equal diversion of kinetic energies resulting from this diverse motion. In other words, whatever kind of motion a molecule executes, the corresponding energy E will be equal to the product of a universal constant k (called "Boltzmann's constant") times the temperature T:

$$E = kT$$

From this, physicists were able to theoretically calculate an important dimension, characteristic of various gases, and what their specific heat would be. This calculus is in agreement with experimental measurements. It was even possible to extend the calculus to the case of solid objects and confirm the Dulong-Petit empirical law according to which specific heat, related to the atom-gram, is the same for all solids (6 calories per degree).

If the foundation of the kinetic theory of gas is based on Newtonion Mechanics, the theory nevertheless did introduce a new concept in physics: the idea of probability. Attempting to follow each molecule in its tormented trajectory through its successive shocks would be an undertaking impossible and devoid of interest from a scientific point of view. On the other hand, it is important to know the average length of the trajectory between two successive shocks, or the average number of shocks sustained by one molecule per unit of time, or other average measurements of this nature. On our scale, the pressure and the temperature of a gaseous sample are average values which relate to a great number of molecules. Presently the kinetic theory of gas is part of the more complete structure of Boltzmann, Gibbs and Einstein's statistical mechanics. The fundamental difference between purely mechanical processes which are always reversible, and thermic phenomena which are most of the time irreversible could thus be logically established. In effect, mechanical phenomena are in principle reversible, for they are able to occur in reverse and time plays no role. Thermic processes, on the contrary, are as irreversible in principle as the equalization of two different temperatures. If the theory of gas, although based on reversible mechanics, declares certain thermic and other phenomena irreversible, it is only able to do so by virtue of the hypothesis of a molecular chaos. In effect, in a gaseous mixture with molecules of varying speeds, how will one select those which are particularly rapid in order to make up a sample of "warm" gas? And in the light of the statistical methods which are concerned with averages rather than being preoccupied with the individual motion which escapes any precise determination, the abstract notion of entropy appears under a new aspect. Thus Boltzmann could establish a connection between entropy and probability, a relation which became one of the most brilliant conquests in all of present-day physics. Boltzmann's system is proportional to the logarithm of its "probability of state," P, which is written:

$$S = K \log P$$

the factor of proportionality being Boltzmann's universal constant K whose numerical value was calculated by Planck in his theory of black radiation. Thus the increase of entropy which is the object of the second principle of thermodynamics simply expresses the fact that the whole system, abandoned to itself, tends toward a state of maximum probability. Now, as any state of probability is close to states which aren't much less probable, one will not fail to find (and this is the new and major thing) systems presenting more or less great deviations and variables in time in relation to the most probable state. This is the kind of thermodynamic fluctuations which are used to explain, among other things, the molecular motion discovered by Brown; it is the disorderly motion of microscopic particles suspended in a fluid which is also observable in the absence of any non-homogeneity of temperature; thus it is a motion of undoubtedly thermic origin. Brownian motion, as well as many other fluctuating phenomena, constitutes one of the most remarkable proofs of the molecular and atomic theory of matter.

Furthermore, the atomic concept is also right in electricity. Thus in the discharge of gases in the phenomena of electrolysis, and in the Zeeman effect, one finds "atoms" of electricity which are electrons and positive ions. Lorentz and Larmor lead the emission and absorption of light back either to the phenomena of vibration (belonging in atoms or molecules) or to the thermic motion of electrons responsible for electrical conductivity in metals.

However nothing contributed as much to the transformation of the atomic notion as the discovery of radioactivity. Inspired by Roentgen's major discovery of X-Rays (1895), Becquerel succeeded in giving evidence of a similar radiation in a uranium cell, and inaugurated the era of nuclear physics.

The fruitful cooperation of thermodynamics and physical optics conceived as a branch of electrodynamics led to one of the greatest revolutions in physics.

Kirchhoff made the major discovery: in any cavity entirely surrounded by walls maintained at the same temperature a thermic radiation of a universal nature — called black radiation — is produced which only depends on the temperature of the walls and not on their physical nature. What's more, the intensity of the thermic radiation of any object can be brought back to this black radiation on the condition of knowing its absorption and its refraction index. In order to study this black radiation Lummer and Wien imagined an ingenious stratagem: they watched what was happening in the cavity through a small hole pierced in the walls, an opening which didn't effectively disturb the state of the internal radiation. This stratagem allowed them to study the nature and composition of black radiation.

If Kirchhoff's discovery went unnoticed for a long time, the attention of his contemporaries was much more attracted to another discovery made by Kirchhoff and Bunsen: black rays in the sun's spectrum coincide with the emission of rays from gas and known terrestrial vapors. It could be concluded that extraterrestrial matter is composed of the same chemical elements as terrestrial matter. The introduction of this spectroscopic method to physics later allowed the deciphering of the innermost structure of atoms and molecules by the very study of the messengers which are the spectral rays emitted by the matter.

But strangely enough, the connection of this discovery to thermodynamics turned out to be less narrow than Kirchhoff had thought: his hypothesis that the emission of spectral rays is made at the expense of thermic energy was erroneous. In most cases it is the electrical and chemical agitation which produces light in gases; in this case the temperature of the radiation greatly surpasses the temperature of the emitting gas. The coincidence between the rays of emission and absorption belongs in the end to the phenomena of resonance, the interpretation of which would ultimately constitute the theory of quanta.

The second decisive stage in the study of the nature of black radiation was accomplished by Boltzmann who, applying the thermodynamic notion of pressure, temperature and entrophy, to the black radiation in the same bold fashion, demonstrated that the density of energy u of the latter was proportional to the fourth power of its temperature (the Stefan-Boltzmann law):

$$u = \text{const. } T^4$$

This was also one of the most shattering triumphs of the electromagnetic theory of light.

The Stefan-Boltzmann Law relates to the energy of the

entire spectrum. It remains to be known what the distribution of energy is in the spectrum's frequencies. The elucidation of this problem marks the third stage in establishment of the theory of thermic radiation.

It was overpassed by Wein with his law "of displacement" which allows one to calculate the distribution of energy for any temperature on the condition of knowing the distribution of a single temperature. Among other things, this law explains why the maximum intensity of the spectrum moves, when the temperature increases, towards the shortest wave lengths, and therefore why the thermic radiation is invisible at low temperatures, while around six thousand degrees, this maximum falls into the spectrum's visible band, to the point that the location of this maximum enables one to measure the temperature of the radiating source, for example the surface of the sun. It was revealed that the law of displacement represents the maximum that we can draw from classical physics. In order to go further it was necessary to call on the quantum theory.

The principal problem, that of representing the intensity of radiation by function v (nv) and the temperature T, in effect resisted all attempts undertaken in the framework of classical thermodynamic and electromagnetic ideas. All the laws that were deduced — Jeans-Rayleigh's valid for low frequencies and Wein's valid for high frequencies — didn't yield to experimentation and to the facts. Facing this situation, Planck established a general formula by interpolation (bearing his name) which correctly translates the experimental facts of both short and long wave lengths at the same time. It can also be brought back, in some limitative cases; to the laws of radiation established by his predecessors. Planck presented this law to the German Society of Physics at their meeting on October 19, 1900; in spite of the doubts raised at the time, later measurements fully confirmed the universal validity of Planck's formula.

It was understood that the real problem remained to be solved: to theoretically found the law that had been more or less empirically established. Planck succeeded in a masterly fashion. Helped by the broad knowledge of thermodynamics that he had acquired in his memorable work on entropy, he clearly recognized that the core of the problem resided not so much in the formula of intensity itself as in the connection of the energy, frequency, and entropy of radiation to this formula. In the course of this research he thus put the relationship between entropy and probability to use in a highly respected system that had been discovered by Boltzmann and quoted earlier. He was only able to calculate this relationship applied to a system oscillating at frequency v (nv) by referring to the thoroughly innovative hypothesis that this vibrating system is only susceptible of absorbing energy in discontinuous packages, by quanta. And this hypothesis, born, one might say, in spite of its author, effectively gave the correct law for radiation. Now, in order to have it also contain Wein's law, each quantum of energy had to differ from the following one by a value of hv, where h is a new universal constant (Planck's constant) which represents the quantum of elementary action. In these conditions the theoretical formula of radiation was identified with the correct formula obtained empirically by interpolation. The comparison of the measure furnished the value 6.5×10^{-27} erg-seconds for h and 1.37×10^{-16} erg-degrees for Boltzmann's constant k, which equally plays a major role in this formula by reason of the very use of Boltzmann's relation of entropy-probability. These major results were the subject of Planck's report, again given before the German Society of Physics on December 14, 1900. Quantum theory dates from that memorable day.

Let's add that Planck's quantum hv of energy doesn't represent a single extension or a natural extrapolation from the physics that are called classical; on the contrary, it marks a profound and revolutionary transmutation in the science. To which point was this revolution profound, and necessary? The ultimate development of all physics, demonstrated it through the following decades: among other things, the quantum idea allowed for the penetration of the mysteries of intra-atomic structure, unveiling its innermost secrets.

If quantum physics, which is characterized by this intervention of the quantum of elementary action h, as well as by the definition of the state of the physical systems by whole numbers, thus appeared at the dawn of the twentieth century, its experimental roots are deeply entrenched in the physics of the last century. The measurement of thermic radiation which led to the change of thought in physics is dated from the last decades of the nineteenth century, and so are the photo-electric effect, the discovery of rays and spectral bands, the variation of the specific heat of certain substances with the temperature, etc. The champions of the old physics hoped that they would be able to interpret all the phenomena on the familiar grounds laid by the old principles. They held physics as a closed, completed, and in a way exhausted science, where only secondary problems, almost without interest, remained to be resolved. So one can easily understand the small amount of attention received in the beginning by Planck's new theory of radiation; the idea of variations of the discontinuous energy was hardly of a nature to excite the imagination of physicists trained in continuous phenomena. Planck himself hoped that he would be able to eliminate the quantum jumps in his theory. The first to recognize the essential, innovative and irreversible character of quantum was uncontestably the young Einstein.

The problem of the reference system of physical phenomena can be traced in the great Hellenic works — Aristotle, Ptolemy, etc. The concepts of position and motion were in effect devoid of sense, as long as no definition was given of the reference system or of the location to which the position and motion could be related . . . the navigator on the high seas needs to find his point in relation to a fixed location, a star or a light. This problem and its analysis has known two major periods, if we set aside the geocentric period — Aristotle and Ptolemy — which takes the earth as the point of origin for a universal reference system. This first period lasted until the seventeenth century; it is the dynamic period which is marked by the shattering and definitive victory of the wave theory of light, and which contains all of physics since the beginning of the last century; finally, the contemporary period of relativity which began with Einstein's treatise in 1905.

We owe the conception of a reference system immobile in the gravitational center of our own solar system to Copernicus; its axis points in the direction of fixed stars, and acts as a reference to which we relate all position and motion. Any system of Cartesian coordinates which serves to locate the diverse points of a physical object is, in effect (except for contrary opinion), related in physics, to this Copernican system;* our dynamic concept of the motion of planets is only possible by taking this reference system as a base. There is a major empirical fact: all the other laws of nature, whether they relate to optics, electricity or mechanics, are presented in this system in a simple mathematical form.

Even though the problem of the reference system had here received a satisfying solution, nevertheless a question of principle remained to be solved. By which right, for what compelling physical reason, would one agree with the Copernican referential system rather than with a geocentric system like Ptolemy's, riveted to the earth? Here, just as in

---

*It is the work in astronomy of Kepler, Galileo, and Newton, which have definitively established the triumph of the Copernican revolution.

his mechanics, Newton (who seemed fully conscious of the major importance of this problem) referred to the idea of "absolute space," space in relation to which equivalence is forever fixed between all correct reference systems. Without being able to discuss any further this delicate question, at the same time epistemological and scientific, let us say that it was the subject of much reflection for Euler (who conceived "absolute" space and time as true physical realities), for Leibniz and, especially, Kant, in the Transcendental Esthetics contained in his *Critic of Pure Reason.*

As physics defines its reference system in view of the objective to be attained, one can, in classical physics, raise this question in the following manner (it is unnecessary to add that these points were only clarified and imposed after great difficulties).

First of all, we must define what it is that we mean by referential or inertial point. A reference system is said to be inertial if any object abandoned to itself describes a rectilinear trajectory in relation to this point. Likewise, we define an inertial time scale such as any object abandoned to itself crossed equal spaces in equal times. According to these definitions, an object abandoned to itself describes a rectilinear trajectory with a uniform speed in relation to the point of inerty. The truth of this Copernican system lies solely on the validity of the experimental facts, because it is simply impossible to observe material points extracted from all exterior influence. The only proof is the perfect agreement of the calculations relating to the planetary orbits, calculations which were based on the mechanics founded on the principle of inertia.

These definitions exclude other kinds of references, for example a system of references which would be animated in relation to a fixed astronomical location by rotational motion. One has known since Newton that an object at rest in relation to a rotating location is submitted to an apparent centrifugal force which is not expressed in the equations of the motion and which simply translates the fact that this object tends to describe a rectilinear motion in relation to a reference which itself would be inert. Thus, if we employ a reference system relating to the earth, and rotating with it, this effect of centrifugal force will appear; it is precisely shown in the flattening of our planet. If a Ptolemaic system of universal coordinates (that is to say, connected to our globe) were adopted, we wouldn't have an inertial system. Experimentally this is made evident by Foucault's pendulum, whose plane turns. Other gyroscopic experiments, moreover, confirm this observation.

Now this isn't the whole story. Already, in his defense of the Copernican system, Galileo had extracted a first kind of relativity. He said that it would be impossible, in the closed cabin of a ship, to infer the motion of that ship, by some mechanical experiment. Mathematically this is translated by the fact that any reference system animated with rectilinear and uniform motion in relation to a given inert point is equivalent in all regards to this inert point. Dynamics thus permits the deduction, from an inert point, of a series of other referentials of equivalent inertia. Newton was already aware of this theorem.

In order to translate the coordinates of an object from one system of referential points into another, animated by a uniform motion in relation to the first, we use simple formulas. Time figures in these, by the same fact of the relative motion of the two reference points, but it remains invariant at the time of the transformation and, in this sense, stays "absolute". For an object in motion, when one measures its trajectory in relation to the first system and then, in relation to the second, one obtains different speeds; however, the acceleration remains the same. The law of motion maintains the same form in the two reference points. And, as no unique system exists which can be used as an "absolute" point of inertia, in relation to which one could relate all the motions in an absolute manner, it is necessary to translate this equivalence in the diverse systems by expressing the Galilean principle of relativity in Newtonian mechanics. This principle asserts that all these reference systems are perfectly equivalent to one another as far as the mechanical description of physical phenomena are concerned; experiments that are purely mechanical by nature are incapable of distinguishing them from one another.

But wouldn't observations or experiments of another type, say optic or electric, bring out some evidence of the existence of a privileged referential system? In truth, one had already thought of the phenomena of optic propagation, the speeds of which could differ according to chosen reference points. Now all the theories of light admitted the existence of an infinitely more subtle medium, penetrating and omnipresent, as the carrier of optic and magnetic effects, a sort of incompressible fluid, ether, which nevertheless escaped any sensible or mechanical representation. Any theory which considered luminous electromagnetic waves as transverse vibrations of this ether were obligated to consider a referential in which this same ether remained immobile as privileged. Thus one thought that one had found an absolute reference point and it seemed to go without saying that this could only be the inert referential of mechanics.

A deeper analysis revealed that under these conditions nothing depended on the speed of the luminous source, nor on the observer in relation to a reference system, but what is decisive, at least in the first approximation, is the relative speed between the luminous source and the observer. Also, the existence of a privileged reference point could only be demonstrated if one was able to observe the influence of a speed common to all affected objects. Now this speed would have to be comparable to the speed of the propagation of light — three hundred thousand kilometers per second —

which is enormous considering our human scale, and if one compares the speed of light to our usual speeds, the relation is far too immeasurable to allow experiment. This is even more important if we consider the phenomena in which speed intervenes by its square; the deviations become completely immeasurable. In the laboratory it is impossible to obtain sufficient speeds for all the objects which take part in the experiment; a speed similar to that of the Earth's around the sun would be required and, even in that case, the relation in question is of the order of 10^{-4}. Anyway, all experiments of this type aimed at detecting the effect of this orbital speed, or in other words, at determining the existence of a "space wind" in relation to the Earth. The decisive experiment was undertaken by Michelson and Morley in 1887. The results were negative: no space wind or wind in "ether" was discovered. The theory of the privileged reference point received its final stroke. The ground was broken for the theory which was going to provide the key to the problem.

We have come to the dawn of the twentieth century. The cast of characters, theories, and facts are in place. The Einsteinian drama is going to develop in the atmosphere of euphoria and happiness of a science that was believed to be complete, where all the problems that we have just analysed in this brief text appeared unimportant, or at least well in the jurisdiction of classical principles, where nothing new or essential could appear. One still does not seem to understand that if science can predict, it can't predict itself.

CHAPTER FOUR

The Relativist Revolution

by FRANÇOIS LE LIONNAIS

It isn't inappropriate to recall that one of the most abstract physicists of all time, Albert Einstein, always manifested an interest in concrete observations, as far as they might be from the icy summits of theoretical physics. We owe a theory of the meanderings produced in liquid currants to this interest; he illustrated the theory with an experiment that anyone can reconstruct in a glass of water. This theory, applicable to winding rivers, allowed for the recognition of Beer's law, in virtue of which the course of water has a tendency to more strongly wear away its right banks in the northern hemisphere and its left banks in the southern hemisphere of our planet. He had a passion for practical inventions, without rejecting the most modest ones, and this did not only happen during the short period when he worked at the patent office in Bern, but throughout all his life. It was in this way that he worked out a mechanical law for fluids, developed by Prandtl, which Flettner was able to apply to navigation by gathering wind in cylinders. Didn't he write, much later, "Caring for man and his destiny must always constitute the principal interest of all technical efforts. Never forget that in the midst of your diagrams and equations."?

However, as revealing of his turn of mind as this work is, it will not weigh heavily in the balance of History beside Einstein's harvest in the field of physics. The least of his research presents itself as a work of art, whose profundity vies with its originality.

One of his first scientific treatises — I believe it was his second — published in 1903 at the age of twenty-three, was devoted to the kinetic theory of heat. Einstein leaned on Boltzmann's statistical concepts and gave a more physical sense to the fundamental relation which that scholar had established between the entropy of a system and the logarithm of the probability of formation of its structure. Surpassing Boltzmann, Einstein discovered the statistical thermodynamics which, unknown to him, Williard Gibbs had just founded the year before.

Brownian motion, this agitation of micelles — or microscopic particles — in colloids, had in the last century become an enigma which had already been resolved, in its principle, before Einstein. It was known that these micelles are agitated because they are exposed to the constant shocks of invisible molecules in the liquid of their suspension. If it is relatively easy to get a global image of this phenomenon, it seems difficult to believe that one could find a mathematical theory of its fluctuations, that is to say, of the light deviations to which it lends itself in relation to the mean. Leaning on the calculus of probabilities, Einstein provided the theoretical solution for this arduous problem, which Smoluchowski, around the same period, had attempted to draft. This solution allowed him to discover a method of calculating Avogadro's number,* which the most various experiments have never stopped confirming. The theory of fluctuations no

---

*That is, the number of molecules of a fixed volume of any substance in a gaseous state, in the given conditions of temperature and pressure.

doubt contributed more than all the arguments already existing to convincing the still reluctant physicists at the beginning of the twentieth century of the reality of molecules and
atoms.

Completing Barnett's discovery of the inverse gyro-
magnetic effect — a solid which magnetizes itself when it is
made to revolve on itself — Einstein and de Haas demonstrated, in 1915, that a solid tends to revolve on itself
when it is magnetized. This experiment confirmed Ampère's
hypothesis which saw every elementary magnet as a gyro-
scope — and, also in particular, considered that any atom
constituting any piece of matter behaved in the same way.

At the moment that Einstein entered the scientific arena,
the quantum theory (Max Planck, 1900) had made its appearance. Einstein immediately recognized its explicative
value and didn't cease to refer to it and employ it in contrib-
uting to increase its importance in physics. In 1907, starting
from the idea that the atoms of solids oscillate following
three directions and applying the quantum theory to these
vibrations, he drafted an evaluation of the specific heat of
solid bodies and established a quantum theory of the law of
decrease of specific heat in relation to temperature.

Each of these works — which we have not tried to recall
in their chronological order — would have been enough to
ensure a physicists' fame. The notion of photons which
Einstein called quanta of light or particles of radiant energy,
which dates from 1905, surpassed the others in a still more
shattering way. While conserving the undulatory interpretation of the phenomena of diffraction and interference in
classical optics, Einstein related a corpuscular image to this
interpretation in order to understand the energetic manifestations of light. The energy of a radiation doesn't distribute
itself uniformly and in a continuous manner in its wave, as is
the case with sound waves; it is localized in certain places
which behave like projectiles. Each photon is the carrier of

an energy proportional to its frequency, the coefficient of proportionality being precisely Planck's quantum of action. The photon theory furnished a correct interpretation of the phenomena of fluorescence (governed by the Stockes law), of photo-ionization and finally provide the key to photo-electric effect, discovered in 1887 by Hertz, which inter-venes in so many modern technics, from photoelectric cells to television. At the same time, Einstein discovered the fundamental law of photochemistry, in virtue of which each absorbed photon provokes an elementary chemical process; this can be verified, on the condition that secondary reactions don't mask the principal effect. But Einstein was mainly clearing the ground for an ondulatory wave mechanics of matter — which Louis de Broglie would soon develop — mechanics which, instead of relating a particle, the photon, to the light wave, guides the particle by means of a wave; this is the Broglian Wave which, since Schrödinger's work, bears his name. Thus developed, wave mechanics conferred all its generality on the dualistic concept of the physical world.

After having brought the photon to life, Einstein, de-veloping a discovery made by S. N. Bose, endowed it with his golden rule in 1924: statistics in virtue of which photons (as well as other particles of complete spin) are immeasura-ble and may form unrepetitive combinations, as opposed to two other categories of particles: molecules, and even human beings, which obey the classic statistics of Gibbs-Boltzmann, and electrons, protons and neutrons, which obey the Fermi-Dirac statistics. These statistics had allowed Bose to recover Planck's fundamental formula relative to the radiation of a black body; Einstein extended it to the phenomenon of degeneracy in perfect monoatomic gases, a phenomenon which indicates the deviation of their behavior in relation to the classical law. He also brought to light the primordial role of Planck's quantum of action in the interpretation of the properties of matter close to the absolute zero.

Finally, in an article of just a few pages, which was published in 1917 in *Physical Zeitschrift*, an article which went almost unnoticed at the time, Einstein put his finger on a phenomenon the principle at which had already germinated in Planck's law and which, a half-century later, was going to find unexpected and sensational development — stimulated emission.

When — for one reason or another — an electron changes energy in an atom and "climbs" to a superior "stage," it won't stay long in this situation and it will "fall back" on its own to its natural level of energy, while emitting a photon. But it will do so at any time without one being able to predict when this phenomenon will take place. This is a "spontaneous emission" of photons. But we can attempt to organize this anarchy by sending, from the exterior, a photon of a suitably chosen frequency. By projecting such a photon against an excited electron, the electron will come back to its initial energy level, in a way on command. The photon emitted at this instant, as well as the photon which stimulates this emission, will be in the same phase. More precisely, the waves which can be related to them will be in the same phase.

This phenomenon, correctly described by Einstein, was to remain in the domain of the laboratory for more than three decades, until Alfred Kastler, in 1950, discovered the technique of "optic pumping" which allows one to obtain a great number of excited atoms. In 1954, reconciling the two ideas and completing them, three groups of physicists (C. H. Townes, Gordon and Zeiger, USA; N. G. Basov and A. M. Prokhorov, USSR; and J. Weber, USA) invented the maser which, in its extension, was at the origin of the brilliant career of the laser.

But this diversity must not conceal Einstein's concern with synthesis. This need for unity is brilliantly shown in his

essential contribution to modern physics: the Theory of
Relativity. Or rather it is a succession of theories, because
the development of Einsteinian thought presents itself as a
series of constructions in which each one by expanding the
former, passionately aims at a permanence beneath the mul-
tiplicity of appearances.

We know of the origin of this revolution. The end of the
nineteenth century had seen the unsuccessful attempts to
prove the motion of luminous sources in relation to ether.
First on this long line, Michelson's and Morley's experiment
dates from 1881. Its result was thought to be scandalous. Let
us imagine a light source, a flame for example, which sometimes moves following a rectilinear and uniform motion and
sometimes remains immobile in relation to an observer; how
can one believe that an observer will see the light propagate
itself at the same speed in both cases? The father of the
electron, H. A. Lorentz, had tried to conjure all this sorcery
by imagining with Fitzgerald that objects in motion shrink in
the direction of their trajectory. This hypothesis was put in
storage with other outdated ideas, but "Lorentz transformation," which is its mathematical expression, has been preserved. Albert Einstein's profound genius had to disengage
itself from all the ideas of the past. In 1905, burning what
physics had honored, he honored what physics had burned:
out of the failure of the Michelson-Morley experiment he
created the principle of Special Relativity.

The universal laws of physics — and not only the laws of
mechanics but also the laws of electromagnetism — are
independent of a uniform rectilinear motion involving referentials (through which the law of inertia is verified), observers and phenomena. Mathematicians say that the laws of
nature are "co-variants" in relation to such motion. Parting
from this single principle, we immediately rediscover the
formulas of Lorentz transformation, but in a manner infinitely more revealing: forming a group, these formulas be-

come the guarantee of invariances for Maxwell's equations governing electricity and magnetism. In fact, these formulas could have been directly deduced even before the Michelson-Morley experiment triggered the alarm. With his equipment and laboratory, each physicist can construct his own Galilean-Cartesian reference system to which he can relate all his observations and measurements. The Lorentz-Einstein formulas constitute a universal dictionary which translates the physicists' results when they communicate them, and gives evidence of the common truths expressed in different languages.

The principle of Special Relativity — so named because it maintains a restriction concerning referential motion — dealt a series of crushing blows to the scientific and philosophic thought of our time.

Classical mechanics and physics became, from then on, only an approximation of Special Relativity, valid only at low speeds. Speeds no longer increase themselves; they are made in a way that the resulting speed can never go beyond the speed of light in a void. An example — which we choose intentionally from daily life to stress its paradoxical character — will demonstrate just to which point this law was in direct opposition to common sense: let us imagine a train moving in a straight line at a speed of 100 kilometers per hour in relation to its tracks. A passenger moves through the aisles towards the front of the train at a speed of 4 kilometers per hour in relation to the train. What will be the speed of the passenger in relation to the railroad tracks? Common sense tells us that it will be 104 kilometers per hour. Einstein's formula tells us that it will be slightly less and tells us in which precise proportion. If the train were moving at the speed of light and if the passenger moved equally through the train at the same speed mentioned above, he wouldn't be moving at a speed superior to that of light in relation to an observer on the embankment. This of course explains the negative result of the Michelson-Morley experiment.

This speed of light — or rather, to give all its generality to the principle, the speed of energy in a void — represents one of the keystones of new physics and appears in a great number of formulas. In particular, in the famous "constant of fine structure," it serves as a link between the electrical charge of an electron and the quantum of action. It is constant and independent from the emitting source. Electroptic ether, the famous "subject of the verb *to wave*," became a useless hypothesis and was abandoned. If the electrical charge of a given mobile material is not altered by the motion of this mobility, its mass increases with its speed; at the speed of light it would become infinite. But on the contrary, phenomena which are not related by causality are perfectly able to separate from each other — as the blades of an opening scissor and at a speed superior to that of light.

This variation of mass with speed brings out consequences of an incalculable importance. In the first place, matter can be transformed into energy, and the same reciprocally; thus one should no longer consider the two principles of conservation of mass (Lavoisier) and of conservation of energy (Mayer) as really separate. It is necessary to unify them into a unique principle of the conservation of "mass-energy." This equivalence of mass and energy is expressed by the famous formula:

$$E = M c^2$$

M measures the mass of any quantity of matter and E the energy that would be obtained in completely suppressing this mass, c representing the speed of light. Notice, on this subject, that it is incorrect to closely relate, as we so often do, this major discovery to the production of the atomic bomb and the disaster of Hiroshima. In fact, Einstein, if he did draw President Roosevelt's attention to the enormous military possibilities opened by nuclear fission, never personally participated in the technical creation of the bomb. Present atomic bombs, of whatever type they are, only transform a small part of their mass into energy, and the phenomenon which was, in effect, explained by Einstein's relation would at any rate have been discovered a short time later by atomic physicists. Parallely, as the combustion of carbon and wood is better explained by Einstein's relation, men didn't wait for the Theory of Relativity in order to discover fire. Nevertheless, this law of equivalence explains many phenomena. It explains the "packing effect" or loss of mass, which is produced at the cost of destabilizing atomic cores. In 1937 W. Braunbeck brought out a new and ingenious proof of this "fault in the mass" by calculating, rather precisely, the speed of light after the losses in mass accompanying the reactions of nuclear chemistry — the transformation of lithium into helium, etc. Einstein's law of equivalence is also found in astronomy: it is because matter is a reserve of energy that stars are able to radiate so intensely and for so long.

Moreover, space and time lost their metaphysical aspects. It is impossible to make them pure products of thought or — as with Newton, who saw them as vacuous frameworks — independent scenery for actors. They are attached to the actors, they are actors. They are revealed by experiment, in the same way as acetylene or electrical potential is. One cannot artificially dissociate them the way one dissociates, for the convenience of daily life, length, bulk and height from technical description or geometrical analysis; in reality they are tightly united as a whole in four dimensions: space-time, or continuum (Minkowski, 1908). If length, volume and duration lose dignity in this — as they are relative to the speed of objects and as each observer sees them according to a different perspective —, their union forms a new absolute: it is the "interval of the universe." The "line of universe" of a particle is formed by the grouping of all its moments — past, present and future — and its positions which are woven in its existence. It doesn't depend on motion — an Einstein-Lorentz transformation doesn't modify it — and it has nothing to do with the physicist's situation.

By a penetrating analysis of the notion of simultaneity (which separates the antecedent-consequent relation from the cause-effect relation without jeopardizing the principle of determinism), Einstein demonstrated how much the past and the future are relative things, the word relative used here in its usual sense and not as in the Theories of Relativity. Speaking of the order of succession of phenomena doesn't make sense for causally independent phenomena. Just as it is with volume, the duration is a local property; it varies with the speed of moving bodies. A clock only measures its own time and that of all the objects in relation to which it doesn't move. Traveling quickly makes life pass more slowly. Time would stop its flow at the speed of light. Let us briefly recall a story which will only make this notion more apparent without essentially changing its content — what this dilation in time could mean, a dilatation which was first explained by Langevin in 1912.

Let us imagine that men are moving away from the Earth, in an appropriate vehicle, at a speed slightly inferior to that of light, for example 299,850 kilometers per second. At the end of about 9 trillion kilometers, which is sixty thousand times the distance between the Earth and the Sun, the space ship turns around and comes back toward our planet at the same speed. What a surprise for the passengers, on their return, at least if they didn't know of the Theory of Relativity or if they didn't believe in it, to discover that their contemporaries have disappeared and that History has advanced about two hundred years. However, they themselves have only aged two years. The needles of the chronometers with which the travellers would have provided themselves would have made one thousand four hundred and sixty turns, while the needles of identical chronometers remaining on the Earth would have made one hundred times more, that is one hundred and forty-six thousand turns. All the activities which characterize human life would have followed the same course: the number of heart beats, alternations between waking and sleeping, respiratory, alimentary and menstrual rhythms, duration of pregnancies, habits . . . At the risk of insisting too heavily, let us say that this isn't a question of a paradox more or less comparable to that which deceived Phileas Fogg, making him count eighty-one days for his trip around the globe. The argument put forward by Bergson, which states that they would only have there an effect of perspective, of which the inhabitants of the Earth would be equal victims, can no longer be retained. Langevin's rocket and the Earth do not find themselves in symmetrical conditions. This asymmetry is confirmed by the fact that the space ship — and not the Earth — returns in relation to the group of fixed stars and the observable universe. It confers its absolute character to the experiment. Perhaps it isn't the most disturbing discovery in all history. It does ruin the Kantian theory of space and time, considered as sensible intuitions *a priori*.

If this is a question of a hypothetical experiment, it does exist in cases where the effect was actually observed.

Certain particles, muons, have a life span of approximately 2.2 microseconds (that is 2.2 millionths of a second), at rest or in slow motion, after which they disintegrate to give birth to an electron or a neutron. We know how to produce these muons in large particle accelerators, but we also encounter them in cosmic rays. They form, then, at an altitude of several kilometers and come to the ground after having crossed these distances at a very high speed, which we know how to measure. With a life-span of 2.2 microseconds and a speed a little less than that of light, that is 300,000 kilometers per second, they ought to disintegrate after about 600 meters and on the ground we should only be able to gather the electrons produced by their disintegration. In fact, they do arrive on the ground, where they are detected by our equipment, having hardly aged since their birth, although this birth has only taken place 30 microseconds, Earth time, before. Their time has been contracted by their speed.

A physicist no longer seriously contests the Special Theory of Relativity. Too many proofs, coming from too many different horizons, corroborates it. The refutations which still appear occasionally now only belong to Science's chronical sense of humor.

The General Theory of Relativity came fully armed out of Einstein's meditations between 1912 and 1915. It postulates that the laws of the physical universe are independent of any motion involving referentials, observers and phenomena, that is to say, co-variants in relations to all motion. Just admitting this principle is enough to deduce from it a new figure in the universe.

The equality of weighty mass and inert mass, already noted by Newton and experimentally verified by Eötvos, led Einstein to locally identify the force of gravitation with acceleration. This leads to saying that the effects of gravitation are identical to the phenomena that we would be able to observe in an accelerated laboratory situated in space, far from all gravitational influence. By obliging the force of gravitation to come out of its splendid isolation, Einstein reduced it to being only a curvature of space-time with regard to the neighboring masses. Lines are no longer straight but geodesic — that is to say lines of shorter distance which follow light rays and material mobiles when their motion is commanded by their sole force of inertia. Newton's co-efficient of gravitation was dethroned by Einstein's ten potentials. The speed of gravitation — which Newton believed was infinite — is the speed of light. Energy, because it is identical to mass, also possesses inertia and, consequently, is as heavy as inertia; a ray of light and an object, or even two rays of light, mutually attract each other like two pieces of matter. Although unlimited, it could be that our space isn't infinite. If this last supposition is confirmed, the mass of the universe would be finite. Gravitation alters the passage of time. Special Relativity and classical physics are only approximations of General Relativity, valid only outside of very intense gravitational fields.

The experimental proofs of General Relativity do not have the irresistible weight of those concerning Special Relativity. Nevertheless, they are impressive. The deviation, 43″ per century, of the perihelion of the planet Mercury — which troubled astronomers — is found quantitatively.* The deviation of stellar light rays passing close by the sun has been confirmed during favorable times such as instances of total eclipses of the sun. We have known, for a little less than a century, of stars which are much more massive and much denser than the Sun and which are, consequently, the seats of much more intense gravitational manifestations. These are the "White Dwarfs" whose densities are between 10^6 and 10^8 grams per cubic centimeter.

In the past few years the astronomer's panoply has been enriched by even more extraordinary objects: quasars. Situated in the confines of the universe, they break all the records of known density and emit — in the form of Hertzian or visible radiation — enormous quantities of energy. There is still much discussion on the subject of this energy's process of production. Certain theories have led us to imagine that the density of quasars engenders a gravitational field so

---

*The Einstein effect is especially noticeable in Mercury because it is the planet closest to the enormous mass of the Sun and, from this fact, the one with the greatest speed of revolution. But we have recently verified the existence of analogous deviations, although much weaker, the Earth and the planet Mars.

intense (much more intense than the field created by nuclear forces) that these objects collapse in a way on themselves in a gigantic "implosion" or "gravitational collapse." Not only atoms are joined, not only are electronic chains precipitated into their cores, but also nuclear forces are overcome by gravitation, the nucleons (that is to say, the protons and neutrons) bounce back into each other. This extraordinary density engenders an Einstein effect so intense that it would be possible that the radiation emitted by certain stars would no longer be able to escape; it would be transformed and trapped in photons. Then objects might exist in the sky which are invisible, in spite of their great density and relative proximity. Finally, there is a last proof: the shift towards red of the spectral rays emitted by masses of enormous density like those of the "White Dwarfs" or that sentinel of astronomy known as the *"Companion to the Star Sirius."* This phenomenon doesn't seem to be able to be uniquely explained by a Doppler-Fizeau effect;* it seems to be necessary to reinforce classical optics with a relativist effect that corresponds to the fact that clocks constructed of very dense materials have a slower sense of time.

But there is something better: the discovery of what is called the Mössbauer effect, allowing us to focus on a proce-

---

*We have the opportunity to observe this phenomenon each time we listen to the whistle of a locomotive speeding past us. If the train were stationary, its whistle would be emitted in its given frequency. If it is in motion, we will first hear a sharper sound — of a higher frequency — as long as the train approaches us, then, abruptly, a deeper sound — of a lower frequency — beginning at the moment when it will pass in front of us. This change is due to the speed of the wave together with the speed of the moving sound source, that is the whistle. This second speed is added to the first in the approaching phase and subtracted as the train moves away. As the train approaches, it attains its maximum at the moment that it is the closest to us, and it decreases afterwards. The same phenomenon exists when we pass from sound waves to light waves. It is indicated by a deviation of the spectrum's color rays.

dure for measuring frequencies with a perfection which, even a few years ago, would have appeared to be miraculous. This procedure is so sensitive that we no longer have to measure the Einstein effect by an astronomical observation, but are able to do it with a laboratory experiment on the Earth.

When a charged particle — an electron in the electronic chain of an atom, or a proton in a nucleus — emits electromagnetic radiation, we know how to measure it with a great deal of precision. Unfortunately this frequency is disturbed by the recoil of the system to which the particle is connected, a recoil analogous to that of a cannon, of the sort which modifies the emitted frequency for the observer; it is a Doppler-Fizeau effect owed to the speed of the recoil of an emitting system in relation to the laboratory. R. L. Mössbauer thought, in 1958, of looking at the crystals in which emitting atoms are fixed, in relation to the crystal, and are not able to recoil at the moment of emission. It is the entire crystal which recoils, with a negligible speed in relation to its great mass. The radiation emitted by a crystal A — in which the recoil of atoms is eliminated — has an invariable frequency, characteristic of the atom of the emitting nucleus. This radiation can be absorbed by another crystal B, identical to crystal A and, consequently, given the same frequency. If, on the contrary, a different wave is sent to crystal B, it won't be conveniently absorbed. This is used in producing a gamma ray from the nuclei belonging to a crystalline A network, maintained at a low temperature. The photon emitted then is then of the same frequency, in the laboratory reference system, thanks to this Mössbauer effect, and it can be reabsorbed by the nucleus in its fundamental state, provided that it be placed in an identical crystal B. Let us put A and B at different heights, that is to say at differing distances from the center of the Earth. Following the Einstein effect, the crystal closest to the center of the Earth or, more practically, at ground level, will slow down in its vibrations, so that its radiation won't be well absorbed because it's put out of phase by the further crystal. But it is easy to re-establish the harmony between the two crystals. It is sufficient to impart the furthest crystal with a certain speed — actually very small — a few millimeters per second. What will result, by the Doppler-Fizeau effect, will be a shift of its radiation towards red. If the adopted speed is well chosen, the engendered shift in the second crystal will be just equal to the shift produced by the Einstein effect in the first crystal; thus the absorption will be perfect and the Einstein effect precisely measured.

Conclusive experiments have been pursued in the United States, the Soviet Union and Great Britain. At Cambridge (Massachusetts), R. V. Pound and G. A. Rebka succeeded, in 1960, in measuring the gamma rays emitted by radioactive iron 57, showing thus, evidence of the different actions of the terrestrial field in two crystals, one of which was twenty-two meters higher than the other! In a distance so small, the predicted and observed shift is of the order of 5×10^{-15}.

The discovery of the Mössbauer effect earned its author the Nobel prize in 1961. Moreover, it hasn't served only as this verification of General Relativity. We dream of applying it to measuring the speed of light in order to understand it more simply, to diverse experiments which put the principle of the Special Relativity into play, as well as the principle of equivalence between the forces of gravitation and inertia, and to numerous chapters in chemistry.

General Relativity is more "general" than Special Relativity, in the sense that it endows physics with a principle allowing the adjustment of laws when the observers and phenomena are animated by any kind of motion, and not just a uniform, rectilinear motion. However it doesn't represent the maximum possible generality in physics. In effect, General Relativity only explains, in a geometric framework, the phenomena of gravitation, while electromagnetic forces remain outside this geometrical framework. Einstein profoundly sensed this disparity and — independently of other great researchers but simultaneously — he devoted himself during the last third of his life to assembling all the known natural forces under this single title. From 1928 on, appealing to the notion of "torsion" in space-time, which completes that of "curvature" and whose mathematical study was done by Elie Cartan, he established the theory of the "unified field," tending to unify not only the gravitational and electromagnetic fields but also the particles endowed with mass and charge which engender these fields, all under the same geometric principle. The solution proposed by Einstein was mathematically correct and interesting, but it didn't yield to experimental proof, which much diminished its worth. Nevertheless Einstein didn't give up retouching his theory, even in his last days. He must have realized, at his death, that the solution to this problem — one of the most fundamental of all physics — is found beyond the horizon.

In effect, the classical fields — gravitational and electromagnetic — which manifest themselves by macroscopically observable effects, that is to say on our scale and on the astronomic scale, have come to be added to the new microphysic fields: the nuclear fields and the fields of weak interaction. On the other hand, the list of particles has been considerably increased, erecting obstacles on the path to unification which, perhaps for a long time yet, will be insurmountable. In spite of their failure, or rather their insufficiency, the efforts made by Einstein and his successors towards unification will have contributed to clarifying physics and to stimulating the great and ambitious research in synthesis.

Another major question remains: that of the reconciliation of the Theory of Relativity and quantum theory, which place themselves respectively, the first under the sign of continuity and the second under the sign of discontinuity. It seems that we are close to touching the goal as concerns the unification of wave mechanics and Special Relativity. But the greatest conceivable synthesis, the one that would explain electromagnetic, gravitational, and nuclear phenomena as well as those of weak interactions by means of a single principle, and which would also show them at the same time under their continuous aspects — their fields — as well as their quantified and corpuscular ones, isn't yet in sight.

Contrary to what the public thinks, Einstein wasn't a great mathematician, but essentially a physician "fascinated by direct contact with experiment," as he himself declared, alluding to his years of university studies. His knowledge of applied mathematics in physics wasn't the less prodigious, and he had the perspicacity to address himself to relatively little-known mathematic disciplines, in order to put them to the service of his ideas in physics.

He brought analytic geometry to its maximum expansion thanks to an idea which he himself named "octopus-co-ordinates" or "mollusc referentials," imaginative expressions which seem to indicate a kind of surrealism and recall Salvador Dali's dripping watches or Raymond Roussel's graduated elastic rules.

Let's take a Cartesian referential, that is to say — and we are considering the geometric plane — the system formed by two axes of rectilinear and rigid co-ordinates, which is familiar to any high-school student. Imagine that we transform each of these rigid axes into a sinuous and flexible tentacle in constant motion; we will have replaced the Cartesian referential with an Einsteinian one. What interest can such a reference system present for a physicist? Evidently it will only be able to be of use if it helps to bring up stable properties, beyond the fluctuations of phenomena and the caprice of its own behavior. This is precisely what it is capable of doing. It isn't difficult to understand why.

Let us imagine that, with the help of this referential, we examine a pure geometric figure, which could be a curve representing an electrical phenomenon or an economic graph. A point situated between two other points on a simple line will preserve this relation of interiority, even if we locate it with the aid of "octopus-co-ordinates." The same way, a closed curve will stay closed, an open curve will stay open. There are truths of this nature — independent of the convulsions of the tentacular axes — which will possibly arise rather poor truths, in a certain sense, and in another sense, major ones because they are occasionally the only ones through which we can hope to trick space-time into yielding us more than just a curve (we will return to this fact in a moment) but also a curvature and torsion which vary very irregularly following the distances in which they are from the different objects.

There is more: not content at having perfected the method of co-ordinates, Einstein succeeded in completely liberating science of the hypothetical nature which constituted this technique, and he furnished it with the means of attaining the absolutes which mathematicians call invariants and covariants. Here I am alluding to the great revolution of mathematics and modern physics: tensorial calculus. Discovered, or rather predicted, in the middle of the nineteenth century by Riemann and Christoffel, rediscovered in Voigt's theory of elasticity, tensorial calculus had been also given powers of infinitesimal analysis and led to maturity by Ricci and Levi-Civita. It was Einstein who opened its doors wide to superior physics.

A tensor is a group of numbers that one can place on a grid and represent by an abbreviated notation, attaching to a letter superior or inferior indexes. In the Theory of Relativity, the numbers defining the tensors are the variables measuring a field of forces. The tensor of gravitation is symmetrical; matter is represented by a tensor with two indexes, its components are transformed in the changing of coordinates. The various theories of relativity request tensorial analysis, which shows itself as being marvellously capable of separating that which is invariant from that which is covariant in phenomena.

The manner in which Einstein put pure geometry to the service of theoretical physics is nonetheless original.

We have said that, in the universe of General Relativity, space-time sees some of its properties change in the neighborhood of material masses. This goes back to saying that it is curved — it is even able to curve to the point of closing in on itself — or that it no longer exists as Euclidean geometry, but as a geometry, imagined a century ago by Riemann, in which we are not able to trace from a point any parallel to a straight line. In such a universe it again becomes possible to square a circle with a ruler and a compass — but only because the words "straight," "circle," "ruler" and "compass" must be understood in a sense different from the commonly defined — and in the neighborhood of a dense star, the number π (which measures the relation of the circumference to the diameter) is no longer equal to 3.1416 . . . Riemann's non-Euclidean geometry is no doubt less simple, for the mathematician, than Euclidean geometry; Henri Poincaré was nevertheless mistaken when he took this state of lesser simplicity as a sufficient reason for forbidding its adoption to physicists. Less simple than Euclidean geometry, Riemann's non-Euclidean geometry is better adapted to reality. A complicated truth is better than a simple error.

Our ways of thinking weigh so strongly in the balance of our convictions that it takes a certain effort to admit that space-time isn't Euclidean — or straight — but Riemannian — and endowed with a positive curve. It is, in our opinion, one of Einstein's highest achievements, that he was able to disrupt the belief in physics (so deeply entrenched in each of us) of a homogeneous space in which all parts are identical to one another and always obey the same geometry. It is in space-time, rendered heterogeneous by the unequal distribution of objects and phenomena — a space-time where curvature or, if you like, geometry, changes in each point — that General Relativity plunges the universe. Its study reinstates Riemann's geometry of space, governed by a system make it possible to measure.

A genius of Einstein's scope doesn't content himself with enriching science while upsetting truths. He conquers these truths according to his own style. Nothing appears more revealing to us of this Einsteinian style than the evolution of the manner in which, in the course of his long career, Einstein resolved the old problem of the alliance between recourse to experiment and the exercise of deductive reasoning.

Certainly one couldn't see any progress in knowledge if one turned our back on facts. Science is above all submitted to facts; such is the guarantee of its infallibility. But isn't it evident that one would hardly ever go forward if one refused to listen to one's thought? If one hadn't occasionally allowed it to go beyond the facts? Science is active reason; this is what most insures it of progress. Thus every authentic physicist behaves according to his temperament by mixing, following a proportion of his own deductive reasoning and the observation of facts. In Einstein, differently from most of the greater physicists with whom we might compare him, the recourse to experiment is less imperious than a call of deductive reasoning. This tendency also developed with the years. In following the history of his work from its origin, in tracing the development of his thought, we notice that the temptation to detach himself from experimentation became stronger and stronger in Einstein with time, and his theories were founded on a deduction that was more and more abstract. From this point of view, the three stages of the Einsteinian relativist construction are very instructive.

It was on the grounds of experimentation — and of older experiments — that the Special Theory of Relativity was established. In contrast, Einstein inaugurated General Relativity by extracting it entirely from his own meditations; it was only confirmed afterwards by several astromic experiments.* Finally, no convincing experiment has come to corroborate the theory of the unified field.

Thus Einstein followed his vocation, further and further reducing the role of experiment and more and more increasing that of deduction. Tending towards something that we seriously attempt to name *a posteriori* apriorism, however, he never went beyond the limits of Science's validity, although occasionally he gave the impression that he might have forcefully been trying to do just that.

---

*We can compare this type of theory, verified afterwards, with the mathematic solution to the phenomena of fluctuations which we mentioned at the beginning of this chapter. When Einstein published it in 1905 he was unaware of how it suited perfectly Brownian motion, which he only learned of the following year.

CHAPTER FIVE

Einstein, the Scientist

by ROGER NATAF
Professor, Paris Faculté des Sciences

Describing the evolution of physics after Einstein raises difficult problems. The great transformation in physics in the twentieth century unfurled under his direction. It is, however, legitimate to say that a great part of the development of this science came after his work, although again in a great part, the developments flowed directly from his work. The situation is that, at a certain moment, Einstein's path diverged from that of most of his contemporaries; in a certain measure, it is a physics contrary to Einstein that we will now discuss.

A stunning example of this evolution is furnished by quantum theory. In his Special Relativity, Einstein had postulated that the laws of nature are expressed by identical equations when we pass from one Galilean reference system to another, provided that each of the physical dimensions figuring in the equations are suitably transformed (in physics one says that it is necessary to submit them to a covariant transformation). This theory was developed in a coherent manner, because the speed of light in a void is a maximal speed, a limit. New dynamics were born, in which the mass of a body varies with speed, where there is an equivalence between mass and energy, following the famous relation:

$$E = M c^2$$

in which this limited speed c appears, becoming a fundamental constant. How could we forget the very important role of this relation in the establishment of the schedule of nuclear reactions which result from the reactions between the elementary particles, neutrons and protons, making up the atomic nuclei? Precisely the formation of stable nuclei from these ingredients is accompanied by a disengagement of energy, which is also shown a loss of mass. The knowledge of such facts, enabled one to predict when the precise isotope of uranium would be submitted to fission under the shock of a neutron, as well as theoretically to consider the chained fission. This is a fundamental and direct contribution in the discovery of nuclear energy, with all its consequences.

In fact, however, this domestication results in the attempted exploration of the atomic and corpuscular domain. For this last, the quantum theory furnishes the precise explanation. Einstein had been a pioneer in the construction of this theory. However its ulterior development and its present appearance have been acquired against Einstein, in opposition to his personal convictions.

This evolution of quantum mechanics deserves to be described.

Huyghens' ideas on the undulatory nature of light had been well verified by interference and diffraction experiments (Newton, Fresnel, etc.) in which the figures of diffraction and interference could be exactly predicted according to the geometric disposition of fissures, diaphragms, etc. Thus we can, through a lens L, transform a light ray into a parallel ray, giving proof of a punctual source A and allowing a rectangular fissure to pierce screen E. After having passed through the fissure the ray is diffracted, that is to say that certain luminous rays are deviated from their initial direction $\vec{z}$, and we can calculate the diffracted intensity in each direction (Fig. 1).

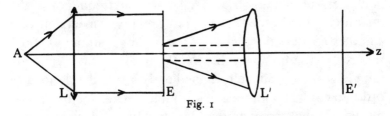

Fig. 1

The physics of waves and fields (since light waves revealed themselves as being identical to the waves of the electromagnetic field) was as determinist as Newtonian and relativist mechanics. In these it was sufficient to know the position and initial speed of a body, the same as the nature of the acting forces, in order to exactly predict the motion, that is to say the position and speed at any ulterior moment. As far as fields were concerned, it is sufficient to know their value in any point of an area isolated in space at one moment, as well as the obstacles in this area (screens, etc.) in order to predict their value at any ulterior moment. In last analysis, this determinism results from the fact that the same causes produce the same effects quantitatively as well as qualitatively; for example, the motion of a point enduring a short interval is caused by the motion during the immediately preceding interval, and the acting force. The motion at a moment t is connected to the motion at the initial moment by a continuous chain of causes and effects. The law of motion in mechanics and the law of the propagation of waves are the quantitative relations between the dimensions of cause and effect. Thus the law of mechanics is expressed: the change of impulsion* during a short interval of time is equal to the product of the acting force times this interval of time.

---

*Recall that impulsion is the product of the mass times the speed. (cf., Chapter 3)

However, Max Planck had demonstrated that the law of thermic radiation of a "black" body would only be explained if we agree to the emission of luminous energy in packages, or quanta. For a light of the frequency ν the quantum is $h\nu$. In the framework of relativist mechanics we can then express the presence of a particle within radiation, the photon, of energy $h\nu$ by the mass*, $h\nu/c^2$ and by impulsion $h\nu/c$; Einstein immediately applied this idea in order to explain photo-electric effect.** This demonstrates, moreover, that the quantum absorbed by an electron which is thus ejected must be localized in a very small area of space, of the order of atomic dimension at the most (being $1 \text{ Å} = 10^{-8}$ cm).

Then if we return to the diffraction experiment in fig. 1, we have to imagine that the light received behind the objective of lunette (lens) L' on screen E' has in any point a proportional intensity to the number of photons that fall there on an average, a relation that Einstein moreover had discovered. But it is necessary to admit that the photons which fall on points different from E' are subjected to different deviations upon passing through the fissure; the same cause produces different effects for each of them and what we can predict is only the average effect for the group of a great number of photons. Einstein vehemently refused to admit that such a probabilist interpretation was definitive, and he thought that the explanation resided in the interaction between these photons in great number.

But Taylor's experiments (1909), confirmed by those of Dempster and Batho (1927) operating with such weak light

---

*It is a question of the photon's mass in motion and not at rest, which is null, its speed being c.

**See the preceding chapter.

that only a single photon could be present at one time in an interferential device, demonstrated soon enough that there was absolutely nothing there. The long-exposed photograph of the figure of interference would remain the same as that obtained by usual procedure.

Moreover, for each individual photon, experiment confirmed the validity of the laws of conservation of energy and impulsion, as Einstein had proposed, in re-examining the law of radiation of a "black" body in the hypothesis of the existence of photon.* This experimental confirmation was supplied by the Compton Effect, observed by H.A. Compton in 1923: a photon of X radiation extracts an atomic electron in changing frequency.

Finally, it would be sufficient to admit, as Einstein had proposed, that the probability of finding a photon in the element of volume dv circling a point M was proportional to the luminous intensity in this point, that is to say to the square of the amplitude of the wave, in order to ascertain that no signal would be transmitted at a speed superior to c, the speed of the propagation of the wave.

The photon hypothesis had been formulated by Einstein in 1905, and until 1923 the double mystery of these undulatory and corpuscular natures of light remained complete. In the meantime, Niels Bohr had formulated his planetary model of the atom (in 1913) by combining, for a planetary electron, the law of Newtonian mechanics and a quanta condition bringing Planck's constant h to intervene. This condition permitted him to select a discreet number of trajectories from among the infinite trajectories possible in Newtonian mechanics. The model perfectly explained the Balmer series of optic rays in the hydrogen atom, admitting

---

*The law of photo-electric effect was already an application of the conservation of energy in the usual process.

another postulate suggested by Niels Bohr: the electron (uniquely for this atom) falling from a quantified orbit, corresponding to energy E′, into an orbit corresponding to energy E, emitted a photon of energy E′−E, that is to say of frequency $\nu = \dfrac{E′ - E}{h}$. Franck's and Hertz's experiments (1914) on the excitation of the atom by electrons confirmed the existence of discreet levels of energy as postulated by Bohr.

Reflecting on the wave-particle duality and on this theory by Bohr, Louis de Broglie thought that it was necessary to associate a wave phenomenon to all particles, among others to the electron. Relativist considerations would demonstrate to him that the length of a wave associated to a free particle ought to be:

$$\lambda = \frac{h}{M\nu}$$

$M\nu$ being the impulsion (M is the mass in motion).

Bohr's stationary trajectories then were able to be obtained by writing that their length was a whole multiple of λ (the condition of a stationary wave).

Moreover he had been guided in his ideas by the theory of analytic mechanics developed around 1830 by Hamilton and Jacobi, which had established the correspondence between a grouping of the motion of particles in a field of force, given to the propagation of a wave in this area of space, and the approximation of geometric optics, that is to say neglecting the phenomena of diffraction (rectilinear luminous rays).

Einstein, informed by Paul Langevin, immediately saw the interest of this work. (answering Paul Langevin, he said of Louis de Broglie: "He has raised a corner of the great veil"). In January 1925 he published a note to draw attention to Louis de Broglie's thesis after having heard the remarks of the Hindu physicist Bose. Bose had demonstrated how the law of the radiation of the "black" body could be attached to a postulate of undiscernibility for the given photons of energy and impulsion (Bose-Einstein statistics).

In the spring of 1926 Erwin Schrödinger tried to pass from the approximation of geometric optics to a strict theory of wave optics for all particles and thus obtained his famous equation.

In the experimental plan, Davisson and Germer, in 1926, demonstrated that an electron beam could be diffracted, like an X ray beam, by a crystal.

Finally Schrödinger demonstrated that his formalism also included that of "matrix mechanics," which had been developed by Heinsenberg and Jordan, students of Niels Bohr, and by Max Born. This last formalism had been imagined in order to obtain a more coherent theory than Niels Bohr's provisional theory: this former hadn't in general, allowed the intensities and polarizations to be obtained from radiation emitted by an atom (except in certain cases, thanks to the principle postulated by Bohr, of a correspondence between mechanics and classical electromagnetics).

Thus, in 1927, physicists were in possession of quantum mechanics, this new mechanics which is applied to the submicroscopic domain of particles.

However, this formalism didn't automatically erase the difficulties in the wave-particle duality; on the contrary it found itself extended to all particles.

Schrödinger thought that the wave aspect solely represented reality, and that the particle was only a package of waves. But we could easily demonstrate, as a result of his equations, that a package of waves localized in time, ought to be extended by propagation in all senses, and the particles would then have to dilute themselves indefinitely in space, contrary to all experimental evidence.

Louis de Broglie imagined a theory called the "pilot wave," in which wave and particle had a concrete reality, the wave guiding the motion of the particle which would be like a characteristic of this wave. But then this would never be manifested except by its action on *its* particle.

Actually, Niels Bohr and his school occasionally maintained rather unclear concepts, founded on the complementarity that we will define later, which brought them to thinking that the particle is the single concrete reality, the registering of all phenomena giving proof of the direct action of the particle: in the case of the photon, it is what is most often absorbed in this process. The wave ought to be an abstract reality giving probabilities for the mechanical states of the particle.

As for Einstein, all his life he opposed this probabilist interpretation, but in a purely negative manner, searching for experiments the interpretation of which were too subtle; he entertained a long controversy with Niels Bohr, whose arguments persuaded almost all physicists, but left Einstein and a few others unsatisfied.* From 1927 on he took refuge in the research of unifying theories of gravitation and electromagnetism: "I must resemble an ostrich who hides his head in the relativist sand in order to avoid seeing these quanta villains," he himself said.

The probabilist interpretation rests on the essentially unobservable character of the function of the wave. Moreover, in the case of a system of particles capable of interacting. Schrödinger had established a wave equation where the wave "propagates itself" in a fictional space whose number of dimensions is equal to those of the co-ordinates which fix the positions of all these particles. This fact demonstrated the abstract character of the function of

---

*Thus, in 1935, Einstein, Podolsky and Rosen published an article in *Physical Review* entitled "Can the Description of Physical Reality by Quantum Mechanics be Considered as Complete?"

(1920) Einstein outside his laboratory in Berlin.

(1930) Berlin. Before leaving for America, Einstein attends the marriage of his wife's daughter, Margot to Dr. Dimitri Marianoff.

(1930) Berlin. The Einsteins leave for America.

(1930) Einstein's first visit to America.

(1930) Mayor James Walker and Albert Einstein.

(1930) Einstein being presented with the Einstein volume of the Golden Book, a permanent part of the Jewish National Fund library in Jerusalem.

(1931) Einstein aboard
the S.S. Belgenland
en route to San Diego.

(1931) The Einsteins
in Panama en route
to California.

(1931) Einstein and his wife at the Tournament of Roses Parade
in Pasadena, California.

(1931) At the Organ Pavilion in Balboa Park, San Diego.

(1931) Einstein, Charlie Chaplin and Mrs. Einstein at the opening of Chaplin's film "City Lights."

(1931) Einstein with other leading scientists. *Left to right:* at the California Institute of Technology, are: Walter S. Adams; Dr. Albert A. Michelson, who measured the speed of light; Dr. Walther Mayer of Vienna; Dr. Einstein; Max Farrand; and Dr. Robert A. Millikan, discoverer of the cosmic ray and president of the California Institute of Technology.

(1931) Einstein
as a teacher.

(1932) Einstein at
a dinner in his honor
at Caltech.

(1932) Einstein
at Palm Springs.

(1932) The Einsteins
return to Germany
from Los Angeles.

(1933) Greeted at his arrival in Los Angeles by Robert A. Millikan, president of the California Institute of Technology.

(1933) Einstein at Palm Springs, California, with film director Ernst Lubitsch *(left)* and critic Samuel Untermeyer. Mme. Einstein seems momentarily unimpressed by the company.

(1933) Albert Einstein and fellow pacificsts meet at the Waldorf Astoria, New York City. *Left to right, front row:* Mrs. Edgerton Parsons; Mrs. Einstein; Mrs. D. Rachel Crowdy; and Albert Einstein. *Left to right, back row:* Mrs. Annie E. Gray; Elmer Rice; Norman Thomas; and Mrs. Ann M. Cohn.

(1933) Einstein at Coq-Sur-Mer, Belgium with his wife's nephew, Fritz Meyer, formerly economic editor of the Berlin "Tagerblatt" before being dismissed because of his Jewish blood. Soon after this photo was taken, Einstein hurriedly moved to England as the Nazi government placed a $5,000 bounty on his head.

(1933) Einstein with Leo Lania whose Nazi bounty was placed at $10,000.

(1933) Einstein and former French premier Edouard Herriot receive honorary Doctor of Law degrees at Glasgow University.

(1933) Einstein with fellow Nobel Prize winners Sinclair Lewis (Literature); Frank B. Kellogg, former Secretary of State; and Irving Langmuir, (Chemistry).

(1934) Einstein in Bermuda,
looking through a glass bottom boat.

(1934) Einstein's first appearance at an American Scientific Conference. Pittsburgh, the American Association for the Advancement of Science.

(1935)
Dr. and Mme. Einstein
on their way to America.

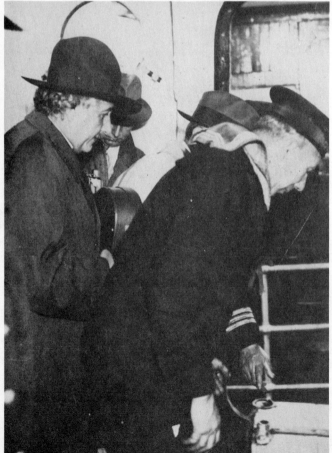

(1935) Einstein arrives in
New York en route to
Princeton, his new home.

(1937) Einstein at Princeton.

Bottom left: (1937) Einstein welcomes his son Albert to New York.

Bottom right: (1936) Einstein with Owen D. Young, head of General Electric at Albany, New York.

(1938) Einstein in his study in Princeton.

(1939) Albert Einstein takes oath of allegiance with his daughter *(right)* in Trenton, New Jersey.

(1939) Einstein at the dedication of the Palestine Pavilion at the World's Fair, with his sister Maja Winteler-Einstein.

(1940) Einstein addresses American Scientific Congress.

(1941) Einstein making a rare concert appearance to benefit the American Friends Service Committee for Refugee Children. He's accompanied by Gaby Casadesus, wife of the French pianist, Robert Casadesus.

(1941) Einstein conversing with students.

(1945) Einstein with Rabbi Stephen S. Wise, president of the American Jewish Congress and World Jewish Congress.

(1943) Commemorating the 400th anniversary of the Polish Astronomer Copernicus where American scientists and one Chinese scholar were honored at Carnegie Hall. *Left to right:* Dr. Henry Noble MacCracken, President of Vassar College and of the Kosciuszko Foundation; Professor Albert Einstein; Dr. Harlow Shapley, Director of the Harvard College Observatory; and Dr. James Y. C. Yen, of Chungking, China. Prof. Einstein and Dr. Yen received citations.

(1946) Einstein at home in Princeton, New Jersey, at the time he announced his support of what was to be Brandeis University in Waltham, Massachusetts.

(1947) Einstein with former Vice President Henry Wallace, columnist Frank Kingdon, and Paul Robeson.

(1948) Mme. Joliot-Curie and Albert Einstein.

(1949) Mrs. Indira Gandhi, Albert Einstein, Prime Minister Nehru, and Mme. Vijaya Lakshari Pandit.

(1951) Einstein with David Ben-Gurion. Einstein was offered the presidency of Israel after the death of his friend and fellow scientist, Chaim Weizman, but he declined saying that he was more familiar with scientific than human relations problems.

(1951) Einstein illustrating his liveliness on his 72nd birthday.

(1951) Einstein buys the 200,000th Israel Bond from Yael Sharett, daughter of Israel's foreign minister.

(1952) A 15-year-old Los Angeles high school student, Johanna Mankiewicz, sent Einstein a request for help in solving a problem. This diagram was his answer.

(1952) Einstein dressed for the New York winter.

(1952) Einstein in a rare broadcast interview.

(1953) Einstein on his 74th birthday.

(1954) Einstein's 75th birthday.

(1953) Albert Einstein on his 74th birthday presented with a model of the Albert Einstein College of Medicine by Dr. Samuel Belkin *(left)* President of Yeshiva University and New York State Attorney General Nathaniel Goldstein.

(1954) Einstein as he approached his 75th birthday.

(1954) One year later, on his 75th birthday, the college is now under construction.

(1955) Einstein's study at Princeton.

the wave. We can also see this in most of the simple experiments which follow; let's take a diffraction experiment, simplifying Fig. 1 in supposing the fissure replaced by a hole, and screen E' by a hemispheric screen centered on this hole. If we suppose that a single photon coming from A falls into this hole, we only know that we will have a hemispheric wave at the exit. If we register the impact of the photon in a point of the screen,* the photon, once absorbed, will cease to exist as well as its wave. If it had a concrete character, it would then be necessary to admit that the absorption of the photon in P would immediately launch its destruction in all the hemisphere compromised between E and S, which can be extended, and this would be contrary to the propagation of any signal with a speed inferior to c.

However the function of a wave of abstract character plays a fundamental role in the calculation of the probabilities of localization of particles. It isn't because screen E is an obstacle to its real propagation that we have the phenomenon of diffraction, it is because this wave function ψ must be immediately nullified to the right of the screen (except for in the fissure) since the particle won't be found there; its probability of localization there is null.

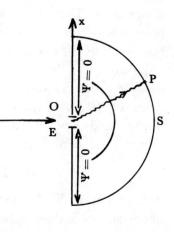

Fig. 2

---

*This will show up on photographic film or, better, it can be materialized by an assembly of photocounter tubes.

Moreover, this example had been given by Einstein during the Solvay congress in 1927 which honored the triumph
of the ideas coming out of Bohr's school. His argument was
that if the photon manifested itself in P and had passed
through O, it ought to have a trajectory between O and P.
Now, the interpretation by Bohr's school is that this asser-
tion makes no sense because it is unverifiable, even if we
replace the photon (almost always absorbed by the detector)
with an electron, for example. Any attempt to detect its
presence in a point in the space ES causes it to deviate in an
unpredictable manner.

This holds for all experimental analysis that we can make
in microphysics: the ideal experiments (*Gedankeexperi-
ment*) indicated by Heisenberg and Bohr.

The result of the new quantic mechanics is that we
absolutely cannot simultaneously measure certain mechanic
dimensions. Thus, if we want to measure the position of a
photon at one given moment, we can make it pass through a
hole such as O, but then it interchanges with screen E by
impulsion; it is the impulsion that it receives that makes it
deviate from its initial trajectory by an unpredictable
quantity. If Δx is the dimension of the hole in the direction $\vec{x}$ and Δp_x the impulsion received in this direction,
then we can demonstrate the new mechanics as such:

$$(1) \quad \Delta_x \Delta p_x \sim h$$

(where *h* is Planck's constant, and Δx and Δpx are the
uncertainties of the position and impulsion parallel to x after
the measurements).

The relations (1) are Heisenberg's uncertainty relations,
valid for all particles. It is these relations which prevent the
precise statement of the photon's trajectory OP in Fig. 2. In
general these uncertainty relations put the classic method of
mechanics in default, since we can no longer measure the
position and the speed of a particle at the same time and

precisely, given the initials which would be necessary for the prediction of its motion; we also have to renounce the trajectory notion in the microscopic scale.*

We will see how formalism proved the existence of dimensions like x and p_x. Bohr named such dimensions complementary; the precise determination of one excludes that of the other.

The idea of complementarity plays a large role in the philosophic aspect of quantum/mechanics. We often find confirmation that the wave aspect and the corpuscular aspect are two complementary aspects of a particle, but this idea, held for a moment by Bohr and his disciples, doesn't in fact correspond to the probabilist interpretation in which, as we have seen, wave function isn't a concrete reality.

It was Max Born who perfected the system of axioms for the new probabilist mechanics, giving the principle of superposition; the names Bohr, Heisenberg, Pauli and Dirac are attached to the elaboration of this system.

Here we can only give a superficial account of these principles:

There exists a formalism which permits the discovery of possible values for a physical dimension attached to a particle system.

These values can form a continuous interval; this is the case for the impulsion and energy of a free particle, or a discontinuous succession; this is the case for a planetary electron surrounding an atom. So we have quantified levels of energy, the ones that Niels Bohr had found through the "old quantum theory" for a hydrogen atom are thus reclaimed in a coherent manner. Strict calculations became

---

*The reader can find a detailed account of these ideal experiments in *Atomic Physics and Human Knowledge* by Niels Bohr.

possible for the systems of several electrons — the heaviest atoms, molecules, etc.

This formalism made each dimension correspond to an acting "operator" in a possible wave function (the grouping of operations of derivation in relation to the co-ordinates, etc.). The condition that this operator's effect reduces itself to the multiplication of the function by a number furnishes the solution: these numeric factors are only certain possible values or "proper values"; each of them can only be obtained with a wave function, the "proper function" (or a limited group of proper functions). The fundamental principle is that the measurement of the dimension can only give one of the proper values for the associated operator; after the measurement, we say that the system is in the "state" corresponding to this value; it is then "described" by the proper corresponding function.

These mathematical methods had been developed by the mathematician Hilbert, a colleague of Max Born at the University of Göttingen. There he led seminars which have remained famous and in which all quantum physics' great theorists participated.

If we now consider several dimensions, we will have several operators. Let's consider the simple case of two. We will designate the operators by A, B. Two cases are then possible:

−A, B are commutative or "commuting," that is to say that we can obtain the same result by applying either B then A or A then B to any wave function. We designate two proper values determined for A, B respectively by a, b; we easily demonstrate that the operators have a common proper function corresponding to these two values. This function then describes a system for which the physical dimensions represented by A, B have the respective values a, b. That is to say that the values are simultaneously measurable, after the measurement of the system is in the state characterized by the two values a, b as designated | a, b >.

—A and B do not commute; so the physical dimensions are not simultaneously measurable. It is the case as we saw for x and px: any precise measuring of the one disturbs the value of the other in an unpredictable manner. A measuring of A leaves the system in the determined state | a >; if we then measure B, we can find one of any of the proper values b_1, b_2, etc. corresponding.

It is here that a second principle intervenes, that of superposition, which allows us to calculate the probabilities for finding each of these values. It rests on the fact demonstrated in all realized cases, that the wave function | a > (taking the same notation for the state in order to simplify) can always be written as a balanced sum, a "superposition," by | b_1 >, | b_2 >, etc.

$$(2) \quad | a > = c_1 \, | b_1 > + c_2 \, | b_2 > + \ldots$$

The principle is expressed: the respective probabilities of finding the values b_1, b_2, etc. are | c_1 |², | c_2 |²; $c_1, c_2 \ldots$ being the coefficients of the development (2) above.

In fact, the formalism of "equations of proper values" only determined the proper functions to a close numeric factor (and it seems then that the $c_1, c_2 \ldots$ are arbitrary), but for each we can precise the "norm". Thanks to this normalization, | c_1 |², | c_2 |², etc. are immediately, in every case, the sought probabilities; their sum is always 1. In particular, according to the principle, the probability | $\psi(M)$ |²dv corresponds the probability to the wave $\psi(M)$ of a particle defined in each point M, by finding the dv circling M in the small voluminous element. The notation | c_1 |² that we have used doesn't exactly represent the square of c_1 but "the square of its modulus;" it corresponds to the fact that we use imaginary numbers in quantum mechanics, as in the electrotechnics of alternative currents. Without insisting on this point, let us remark that it leads to great simplifications in formalism; notably, the intensities of classic optics analogous to $|c|^2$ are obtained by taking the square of real amplitudes, then their average in time, because they are periodically oscillating quantities; this second operation becomes useless when we consider the imaginary representation.

The principle of superposition had been obtained by an obvious generalization of what is observed in classical optics. For example we can split an elliptically polarized light wave into two waves of rectilinear polarization following two perpendicular directions 1 and 2, by a development of the type (2), limited to two terms. Situating a Nicol analyzer to allow a polarized light to pass in direction 1, we obtain an intensity in relation $|c_1|^2$ with the initial intensity. With quantic interpretation we have seen that the intensities are proportional to the number of photons, therefore to the partial probabilities.

The success of quantum mechanics in the explanation of physical phenomena was considerable as, according to Dirac's proposal, it explains all of chemistry and almost all of physics. This means that Schrödinger's equations cover all atomic and molecular properties and it is sufficient to know how to resolve these equations in order to predict these properties. Just the same, quantum mechanics were successfully applied to the study of solid bodies, with the numerous applications that we know for semiconductors, superconductor bodies of a low temperature, etc. On the other hand, it correctly accounts for nuclei properties such as nucleon systems. The quantum theory of stimulated emission, already sketched by Einstein in the study of the radiation of "black" bodies, was applied to the construction of lasers (see the preceding chapter).

All the theoretic work is based on Schrödinger's equation, and relies on methods of suitable approximation, and on the new statistics applied to elementary particles. Identical elementary particles must be considered as undiscernible when they are placed in the same quantum system, since we can't follow their trajectory there. Bose had applied this to photons, as we have seen above. Apart from *bosons*, which are undiscernible but can be found in any number in a given state, there are also undiscernible *fermions*, but they only exist in a determined state (Pauli's principle of exclusion); electrons and nucleons (neutrons and protons) are fermions. This fact is essential for filling in the electronic layers of atoms and molecules, for the properties of electrons in metals, etc.

Thus, a great part of the technological success of our civilization rests on the application of quantum mechanics. In the face of this situation, Einstein's attitude, isolated and retired in his ideas, seems negative to us. It appears very surprising to us that the creator of the Theory of Relativity, which destroyed the traditional frameworks of space and time, had refused the revolution that quanta brought about in the framework of causality. This fact perhaps came in part from Einstein's very concrete initial change of mind, even though he had pointed to the utilization of abstract formalism. In the beginning, it appeared more concrete to him to substitute photons in waves, since ether, once considered as the support for these waves, disappeared in the Theory of Relativity. However, when he saw the necessity of maintaining completely abstract waves, his mind revolted before the prospect.

Apart from the abstract character of the wave function, philosophic considerations occasionally entered and animated these discussions. In effect, certain members of Bohr's school presented wave function almost as a subjective knowledge on the part of the observer, which implies an

idealist position;* others attributed the phenomenon of complementarity to the act of measuring, which thus takes a
mysterious character. It seems that these misunderstandings
can be completely raised. Thus, the analysis of the measuring process by detective apparatus or detective-registering
material (which are opposed to "generator" apparatus preparing particles in a certain state) demonstrates that these
apparatus act little on the particles, thanks to the great
number of their microscopic elements and a long enough
time of relaxation, they erase certain interferences of the
microscopic scale and thus give measurements conforming
to the principle of superposition.

In any case, it was this confusion which led certain
theorists of materialist philosophy,** or even realist, to doubt
the traditional interpretation of quantum mechanics. On the
contrary it seems to us to extend the framework of relations
from the abstract to the concrete in physics. The concrete
phenomena appear in effect as essentially changing, per-
petually developing, and often very complex. However,
when we make a quantitative analysis in measuring the dimensions, we discover that there are permanent relations of
cause and effect between these dimensions. The laws of
nature are quantitative mathematical relations, necessarily
abstract. These are permanent and more simply bind the
complex, concrete phenomena to their own changes. With
quantum mechanics, we see concrete microscopic
phenomena even escaping causality, but an abstract dimen-

---

*These terms are taken in the philosophical sense: for the idealist,
nothing exists outside of thought, while the realist asserts the existence of beings independent of the mind which perceives them: the
realist can be either materialist, spiritualist (when he admits that the
being is of spiritual essence), or dualist if he admits these two types
of reality.

**See previous note.

sion, the wave function, conserves a strict determinism which allows us to calculate the probabilities relative to the states of particles. On our scale, obviously, determinism makes its reappearance as we observe the means in a great number of particles.* Naturally, it isn't a question of the traditional probabilist interpretation's being opposed to materialism, *a fortiori* to realism, since, as all physics theory, it exists for the sake of explaining the properties of matter. Moreover, whatever the philosophic options of a scientist are, and where his speciality is (excepting mathematics), we can't see, on our part, how he couldn't have a realist position, if he believes in his profession. The same difficulty that he has to change his concepts in extending the domain of his experiments is for him a proof of the reality of the material world.

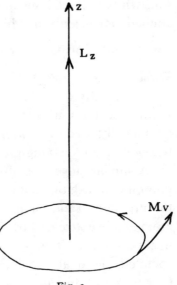

Fig. 3

After this brief reminder of the developments in quantum mechanics, we should now study the importance of relativist covariance in the quantum theory of the electromagnetic field.

Schrödinger's equation is a nonrelativist equation applied to particles of weak speeds. It was at first completed by the introduction of spinning particles. From general formulas of quantum mechanics it resulted that the projection

---

*However, we can imagine experimental apparatus making a macroscopic event depend on the essential hazard of a microscopic event.

on an axis of the kinetic momentum of a system was "quantified" by whole values of $\frac{h}{2\pi}$.

The experiment demonstrated that it was necessary to add to this orbital momentum of particles a proper kinetic momentum, or spin, able to take semi-whole multiple values of $\frac{h}{2\pi}$.

It equally demonstrated that all semi-whole spinning particles are fermions and all whole spinning particles are bosons. In 1926 Pauli indicated the formalism for the spin as ½ applied to the electron, which implies a wave function of two components corresponding to two spinning states $\pm\left(\frac{1}{2}\frac{h}{2\pi}\right)$.

Dirac demonstrated that a wave function of four components perfectly describes a relativist electron: it bring well-verified corrections to the spectroscopic levels in the optic domain (the hydrogen atom) and X (the deep electrons of heavy elements having great speeds).

A similar stage was also necessary in order to treat the photon in a fashion analogous to other particles. However, the problem of emission and absorption of photons by an atom had been treated by Schrödinger, drawing its singular inspiration from Bohr's principle of correspondence; he associated classical oscillating electromagnetic dimensions (expressed by the aid of wave functions of initial and final states of the electron) to an electronic transition. These dimensions were introduced in Maxwell's classic equations for the electromagnetic field, and thus we obtain the intensity and polarization of the emitted radiation, that is to say, by keeping in mind the fact that it carries a photon, we give an account of the probability through the unity of the time of transition, accompanied by the emission of this photon. But this quantification of single material particles isn't satisfying. Thus, an electron unconnected to the atom, broken by the presence of electric forces, emits X radiation (called "the break") whose frequency spectrum is continuous; in this radiation there are, however, photons of all energies susceptible of producing a photo-electric effect.

Also, around 1928, Dirac, Jordan, Wigner, Heisenberg and Pauli attacked the quantification of the electromagnetic field. The same way one goes from classic mechanics to quantum mechanics in associating an operator operating in the wave function to each classic dimension, parallely they considered the fields as operators acting on a "state" characterized by a certain number of photons of each frequency. Thus a field of frequency ν corresponds to an operator destroying the photon of this frequency. An emitting operator is associated to this absorbing operator.

In the absence of charged particles, the evolution of a state is given by a product of these two operators, so that the number of photons don't vary; the energy and impulsion stay constant. From commutative relations established between these operators, it results that this energy and this impulsion are quantified in quanta $h\nu$ and h/λ.

Thus we have the free electromagnetic field formed by photons and "material" particles. We then introduce a coupling term between the two where an operator only figures by emission or absorption in the same way as the electromagnetic current constructed by Schrödinger, associated to a transition of the charged particle; in the transition, a photon is emitted or absorbed. The probability of this process is the same as in Schrödinger's theory and is proportional to the square of the elementary charge e of the particle, or, more precisely, to the dimensionless constant $2\pi e^2/hc$

$$= \frac{1}{137} \text{ (constant of fine structure)}.$$

Thus a theory had been built allowing the precise calculation of the probabilities of emission and absorption, and also all the "classical" characteristics of radiation (polarization, etc.), thanks to the field operators satisfying to the classical field equations. But the former also had the role of explaining the propagation of finite speed in the interaction between two charged particles, a finite speed which enforces the Theory of Relativity: a field is emitted by one of the particles and then it acts on the other. In quantum theory, this field corresponds to a "virtual" non-observable photon exchanged between the two particles and transferring the impulsion from one to the other, so the two particles are diffused. This process is represented in the scheme of fig. 4, or Feynman's graph, which only represents the connection between diverse particles and not the trajectories which aren't definite.

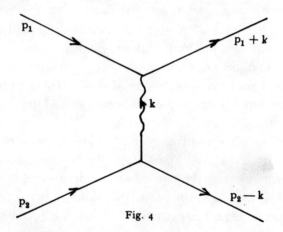

Fig. 4

We then imagine that this theory, quantum electrodynamics, can be changed into any interactions of "material" particles. Any interaction corresponds to a classic field which propagates it and, therefore, by quantification, to a determined particle. We also see that the concepts of "field" on the one hand, and "material particle" on the other, lose their distinctness. It seemed, around 1927, that only field particles like the photon could be created and destroyed in the course of a physical process. In reality, the difference between these two categories held uniquely to the fact that the particles then called "material" had a semi-complete spin, so they could only be destroyed or created in pairs because of the conservation of kinetic momentum.

We also sought, towards 1930, to construct a field theory, for the electron, for example. It appeared that one such theory raised certain difficulties for the relativist quantum equations. We have seen that the wave function of a relativist electron has four components: those corresponding to the two spinning states and to the fact that the relativist energy of a free electron E, connected to the impulsion p by:

$$\frac{E^2}{c^2} = p^2 + M_0^2 c^2$$

(M_0 mass at rest), can be selected positive or negative. Such a state of negative mass obviously hasn't any physical sense, but with a field theory we are led to associate the absorption operators to the "positive" frequencies, and those of emission to the "negative" frequencies, so we can re-interpret the absorption of an electron to negative energy as the emission of a particle of the same mass at rest M_0, in which all dimensions susceptible of carrying a sign have the sign opposed to those of the electron (charge, magnetic momentum, etc.).* It is a question of the anti-electron, or position, predicted by Dirac and effectively discovered by Anderson in 1932 in cosmic radiation. This notion can be extended to all "charged" particles (that is to say having several characteristics provided by signs); thus each particle is associated to an anti-particle, the two being described by the same quantum field. Exceptionally, particles and anti-particles can be identical (case: "non-charged"); this is what is produced for the photon. Thus we see how this anti-particle

---

*It is necessary to note that the commutative relations of the field must be taken differently for fermions on the one hand and bosons on the other.

concept is essentially connected to relativity. Moreover, the electron and the positon, for example, can mutually destroy each other in emitting a photon whose energy is 2 M_0c^2, that is 1.02 MeV if the two particles are at rest (in fact, two photons of 511 KeV); inversely, a photon of superior energy, at an energy superior to 2 M_0c^2 can be "materialized" in a pair of positive electrons. Presently, we are intensely studying the production of mesons, in proton-antiproton destruction, for example. These processes can obviously only be understood in the framework of mass-energy equivalence.

Let us now consider relativist covariance and the "renormalization" of quantum electrodynamics. Electrodynamics predicts processes of superior order where there would successively be several emissions and absorptions of virtual photons corresponding for example to several successive transferences of impulsion between particles. As the probability of the processes doubles, triples . . . proportionately to $\left(\frac{1}{137}\right)^2$, $\left(\frac{1}{137}\right)^3$, etc., we will be able in general to omit them before a simple process, that is to say that the smallness of the coupling constant allows us to treat the quantum problem of coupling in the electromagnetic field and in the charged particle by the method of disturbance. However, if we calculate the process of the second order corresponding to Feynman's graph in fig. 5, that is to say to an interaction of the electron with its own field, we find an infinite result. This isn't new, as we have considered an electron as a pin-point, interacting with the photon when it finds itself at the same point. Its proper energy was then already infinite in the classical case. If we try to introduce an extended electron, that is to say in fact a more non-local, non-punctual electron-photon interaction, we run up against the difficulty that this interaction would be propagated at least in this extension with a speed superior to c for an electron considered as a perfect solid, the speed would be instantaneous from one end of the particle to the other. Up until here this last difficulty with the non-local theory has been unavoidable. Therefore we kept the local theory and outlined this difficulty by working out a calculus to present each stage, in an obvious form, of relative covariance, following the work of Tomonaga, Schwinger and Feynman* in 1944-46. The method consists in saying that the electron's observed mass at rest is the sum of the electron's unknown mass mu (that is μ) and of this proper energy δM, due to the trimming by the equally unknown electronmagnetic field, that is $M_0 = \mu + \delta M$.

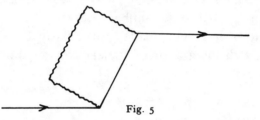

Fig. 5

Introducing the physical mass M_0 at the departure, it is necessary to see whether we can adjust δM to each stage of the calculus in a manner of compensating the terms of proper energy. We recognize these terms, although they are infinite, by their relativist invariance. Applying such a program to the mass (renormalization of the mass) and to the charge (renormalization of the charge), we were able to calculate very small effects with very great precision, like the difference in energy between two levels of the hydrogen atom, which were confused in Dirac's theory but whose separation was made evident by Lamb and Retherford in 1945; it was revealed by a technique employing absorption by Hertzian centimetric waves, and had been afterwards explained by the difference of effects of the proper electromagnetic field in

---

*Which earned its authors the 1965 Nobel Prize.

a linked state and in a free state. In reality it was the observation of this effect which was at the origin of renormalization techniques, whose general significance to all orders was demonstrated by Dyson.

In the model of quantum electrodynamics, we have tried to construct a quantum field theory for each kind of particle, the couplings between these different fields leading to the processes of creation and annihilation. Relativist invariance automatically leads to the customary laws of conservation in classic or quantum mechanics: conservation of impulsion, energy, kinetic momentum. Other laws of conservation ought to be added if we mean to keep the experimental data in mind: charge, baryonic number, etc.

Application has been made, particularly by Fermi in 1936, to the β disintegration of nuclei corresponding to simple processes:

$$\text{(a)} \quad n \rightarrow p + e^{-} + \bar{\nu}$$
$$\text{(b)} \quad p \rightarrow n + e^{+} + \nu$$

p and n designating proton and neutron, e^{-} e^{+} electron and positron, ν, ν neutron and antineutrino. A neutron is a neuter particle of mass at rest null, like the photon, but of one-half spin. Its existence had at first been postulated in order to satisfy the conservation laws in (a) and (b). (a), which is exoenergetic, is possible for the free neutron. In Fermi's theory, the term of interaction contains four fermions and depends on a coupling constant much weaker than $^1/_{137}$ in the considered energies. A disturbance theory is then fully justified, but the method of renormalization doesn't succeed here, the infinite quantities encountered in each stage can't be made to amount to two (mass and charge) as in the preceding case; however, the calculus of the first order always gives satisfying results. An interaction of the same force and probably of the same type is responsible for the disintegration in all elementary particles of "long" average

life discovered since (hyperons, mesons . . .). Since 1957 we
have know that these interactions have symmetric properties very different from electromagnetic interaction: the processes that they engender aren't invariants by spatial symmetry (non-conservation of parity).

On the other hand, the nucleons in the nuclei are connected by very intense but very short range forces. It results
that the quantum of the intermediary field must have a non-
null mass at rest, of the order of two hundred times the mass
of the electron. This is the field that Yukawa postulated in
1935, calling it the mesic field. This meson has since been
identified, with the meson π exist in the forms π^+, π^- (mass
139 MeV), π^0 (135 MeV). Unfortunately, in relation to the
intensity of the forces, the coupling constant $\frac{1}{137}$ must here
be replaced by a dimensionless constant of the order of 15;
any disturbance calculus is therefore excluded, of the sort
that this theory wasn't able to give a truly satisfying quantitative result, although it is renormalizable. On the contrary,
more than the symmetries of electromagnetic interaction, it
possesses properties of special symmetry: the particles of
strong interaction, or hadrons, have quantic internal numbers (isospin, strangeness) preserved by this interaction.* It
seems then that there we would have at least three kinds of
essentially different interactions of properties, incapable of
relying simply on each other. Such a complexity seems to
render Einstein's efforts to end in a single theory for electromagnetism and gravitation illusory.

The following table gives a summary of these three types
of interactions. The crosses indicate that the designated

------

*It is by supposing that the strong interaction breaks apart very forcefully
with a vaster (SU_3) internally symmetrical system of average strength,
that we were recently able to class hadrons in multiplets.

particles submit to the interactions designated at the head of each column.

In fact, we have added yet another interaction much weaker than the weak interactions: gravitation, which (for this reason) isn't practically manifested on the microscopic scale; all particles nevertheless are submitted to this force. Considerations of logical coherence along with uncertainty relations indicate that it ought to enter into the general scheme of the quantum theory of fields; if such is the case, it is propagated through a particle of spin 2, of null mass at rest, which is called a graviton. Like any other particle, the graviton itself is submitted to the effect of gravitation (indicated by the double cross); its free field must therefore be coupled to itself, that is to say to obey non-linear equations, like Einstein's in General Relativity, but then this field can't be quantified by the usual procedures. This is a problem which still isn't clearly resolved.

PARTICLES \ INTERACTIONS	STRONG $G^2 = 15$	ELECTRO-MAGNETIC $\text{"}e^{2\text{"}} = \frac{1}{137}$	WEAK	GRAVITATIONAL
Hadrons { baryons: nucleons, hyperons (Λ, Σ, Ξ, Ω), etc. ; mesons: π, K, etc.	+	+	+	+
Leptons : electron, neutrino, muon		for charged leptons	+	+
Photon		+		+
Graviton (?)				‡

This leads us to the Einsteinian theory of gravitation, which is General Relativity.

Whereas Special Relativity intervenes, as we have seen, in every stage of the quantum theory of fields (whose sole logical and quantitative success, to tell the truth, is electrodynamics), General Relativity remains outside the framework of the microscopic study of matter because the forces of gravity only make themselves practically felt in the macrophysical universe of large masses, such as the planets. It has been seen in the preceeding chapters that gravitation results in the General Relativity of a curved space-time, the principle of covariance being extended to the changing of co-ordinates in such a space. Einsteinian gravitational equations connect the curvatures in this space to the density of the matter present and to its motion. The equations are non-linear in relation to a field of ten components that we can consider as a gravitational field.

To tell the truth, Einstein wasn't satisfied with this formulation and thought that matter in fact ought to result from the field, that is to say that material particles ought to be like a hump (an area of elevated field) in the field. This is what is called a non-dualist theory. Around 1927 he thought he could justify this concept by certain mathematical results then obtained. It was also for this reason that he was opposed to the principles of quantum mechanics as elaborated at the same time; in them, particles are the only concrete reality, a concept diametrically opposed to what Einstein then had in view.

Recently, towards 1953, de Broglie, Boehm and Vigier went back to Louis de Broglie's first theory (the pilot wave), introducing Einstein's idea to it. Since this new attempt, de Broglie has continued in this direction. He considers that the abstract wave of quantum mechanics corresponds to a distribution of concrete waves provided by bosses which are the particles; each boss would have a definite microscopic

trajectory, but at hazard, by reason of unknown mic-
rocauses; quantum mechanics would be a statistical result
like those which we have deduced in the kinetic theory of
gases (incomplete information on the classic motion of
molecules). The spreading of the packages of waves which
resulted from Schrödinger's linear equation wouldn't be
found here for the boss because the wave obeys a non-linear
equation which is reduced only to a linear approximation
outside of this boss. Unfortunately, this theory again brings
up profound difficulties for the pilot wave: if there is a
concrete wave and if we attribute to it real propagation and
the obstacles that it encounters in phenomena of interference,
diffraction, etc., it must sometimes be very extended (at least
as far as tens of kilometers for the Hertzian waves whose
interference we observe in radio-astronomy's interfer-
ometers). Now, it ought to be able to be observed some day in
some manner outside of the boss which constitutes the particle. Otherwise where would it exist concretely?

But then we fall back on the objection raised by Einstein
in 1927 (fig. 2, page 129): the instantaneous disappear-
ance of all this wave at the same time as its boss, should lead
it to the possibility of instantaneous propagation of signals
contrary to relativity. (It is true that this possibility is rather
ideal because it would be necessary to identify a wave.)
Finally, it is necessary to note that quantum mechanics
considers the propagation in real space of an undulatory
dimension* only if we have an isolated particle: but the
"spinorial" wave which is found to be associated to particles
of one-half spin is unobservable, etc.

---

*This "propagation" might seem strange for an abstract dimension, but it
merely insures the speed of the packages of probability of presence,
which are therefore particles, as we have already remarked.

Einstein's supreme ambition was the construction of a nondualist and unifying theory, in a gravitational and electromagnetic geometry.

It is probable that a unification phase will succeed the present period of diversification of the theory through the discovery of dynamics of "elementary" particles, but the general opinion is that this won't prove to be a return to the more classic concepts; on the contrary, it would even further upset the principles admitted until now. For twenty years, in a perspective of this type, with quantum ideas going beyond "dualism," Heisenberg has attempted to unify all known particles and interactions in a unique quantum field satisfying to a non-linear equation, but so far his efforts don't seem to have been crowned with success.

Einstein was the pioneer in physics of our century, from the microcosm to the macrocosm. Constructing his theories of Special and then General Relativity on the ruins of the classic conceptions of space and time, he however refused to see the downfall of causality in microphysics. In this he probably showed a weakness common to all men, that of refusing to change their concepts after arriving at a certain age. This might seem surprising in a man who had been so bold and daring in his youth, but it also demonstrates how this genius was still profoundly human.

CHAPTER SIX

From Pacifism to the Bomb

by PIERRE-HENRI SIMON

Humanism is a word ambiguously rich in its connotations. In this chapter, we will try to analyze its implications in relation to science. In any case, the first connotation which comes to our mind is the humane, and its meaning is simple. Therefore, we will begin by speaking of Einstein's humanity.

I am not about to present a biography, and trace a portrait of the man. However, let us evoke his image, familiar to everyone after the Second World War — for example, as he appeared in his Princeton laboratory: rather badly dressed; the cuffs of his trousers bunching over his big shoes, wearing a loosely hanging sweater, while his attractive, beautiful mass of silver hair framed his inspired forehead and fell almost like a helmet over his head and neck. It was this artist's image which this somewhat bohemian scientist, the most straightforward of men, liked to give. I don't know whether the mixture of shrewdness and ingenuity that shined in his eyes from beneath the raised brows was natural or affected, but it is certain that there was a charm in this man which had much to do with his contradictions: distracted and attentive, easygoing and mischievous, modest and proud, misanthropic and social, he liked to look like an absent-minded professor, but, in speaking of his colleagues, his science, of women, and especially of his own wife, he showed a sense of humor that was in no way naive. Pointing out of the window of his Prague office which overlooked the courtyard of a mental hospital, he loved to say: "That's not the pavilion for people who handle quantum calculations."

In an unusual way, Albert Einstein was the epitome of the humane scientist. Let us look first at the scientist in him: his entire existence was marked with the most generous attitude towards knowledge, a knowledge which was to touch on the most abstract and the most absolute — in the beginning he didn't believe in any possibility of practical and technical use for the equations, which, in spite of their inherent simplicity and subtlety, let to his explanation of the physical world. Honors were piled on to him without ever unsettling him. He thought and said, with less irony than honest realism, that "a scientist ought to earn his living as a cobbler," meaning that he did not have any right to take money for the discoveries which he was not certain of making, but he had to earn his daily bread with humble day to day work — a work which rose from acquired competence rather than from the miracle of genius. He wanted his work to be that of a professor, which he would accomplish with a surprising mixture of conscience and fantasy, completely devoted to his pupils, his collaborators, and, above all, aspiring to an intellectual independence, withdrawing almost haughtily into himself, as he knew that the fortune and virtue of a master were tied to the fact that he would have nothing to offer to others if he neglected the cultivation of his own originality.

Certainly nothing is more humane than a vocation where the mind directs all of its forces to understanding the universe, to uncovering its secrets and discovering its laws. And yet the practice of science can dull the soul, especially when it is applied to organizing material phenomena and expressing their relationships in abstract mathematical formulas. It can close the heart and even the intelligence to feeling and ideas which retain the vibrancy and uncertainty of the biological and moral world. But there was nothing like this in Einstein's character. Philippe Franck, one of the best judges of his character,* noted the importance of beauty for him. Not only had he, as a child and ever after, carefully retained his taste for poetry and music, but also as a professor, his lectures and lessons developed like works of art; his ambition even as a scientist was to interweave both rational and esthetic values through the most vast and flexible theory of knowledge in an elegant and simple framework. We hardly exaggerate by placing this most modern of minds in line with the fathers of Western thought — Heraclitus, Parmenides, and Pythagoras — who advanced metaphysical speculation to a level where it joined the poetic imagination to reduce the totality of the real world to one unifying symbol.

Thus he succeeded in preserving the artistic dimensions of thought in laboratory research through his profound investigation of physics and the practice of the most refined mathematics. Similarly, Einstein did not fall prey to the imperialism of scientists who do not care to recognize anything existing outside of their own field. No doubt it was impossible for him to integrate mysticism into scientific research, but he could occasionally do so with esthetics; he brought both aspects together as much as possible, asserting that the mystical emotions are among the most beautiful that we can experience, and that they spring forth noble and powerful at the discovery of the cosmological order. He came to believe that "science without religion is lame, and religion blind, without science." Moreover, his conception of religion was largely detached from rites and dogma, as he believed in an essential movement of the soul towards the pure idea of God. Despite his Jewish descent, he received a

---

Einstein: His Life & Times.

Catholic education through his profoundly Germanic family. Later he rejoined the Jewish community, but he was never devout and he always seemed to put in doubt the anthropomorphic simplifications of catechisms from which, he said, "Children end up believing that God is a kind of gaseous vertebrate."

He was careful not to cut his scientific mind away from the spiritual world. Einstein thought that the scientist should never let himself be absorbed by his studies to the point of losing touch with the political conditions of his existence and avoiding these responsibilities. Profoundly liberal and already ill at ease in Wilhelmian Europe, he decided, in his teens, to complete in Zurich the studies he had begun in Munich, and remained in Switzerland for ten years, where he began his career as a professor. Then, already a celebrated man at the age of thirty, he went to the University of Prague, in Bohemia, always fleeing from the Prussian militarism that he detested. However, his renown was such that he could not escape the pressure that called him back to his own country. The war found him at the University of Berlin, where, solitary and distressed, he would spend the black years that saw Europeans slaughtering each other. After the Versailles peace treaty had been signed, he threw himself into moral and political action with the authority that the prestige of his studies in relativity had earned him throughout the world. He fought for universal cooperation under the auspices of the League of Nations, for European understanding, and for Zionism; however, his actions may have occasionally lacked in measure and reflection as far as their consequences were concerned — Einstein was always consistent and methodic in his choice of means, but it was always inspired by the hope of creating more order in the world and more peace among men. Because he wanted both liberty and justice at the same time, he was against totalitarian revolution; he was anti-fascist but also anti-communist.

He admitted that his pacifism was intensely emotional, declaring to the U.S. in 1920, "This is the way I feel because I find murder repulsive. I could give you some reason for this reaction, but in reality that would be the product of some afterthought." This was an important confession on his part for it gives us the order of priorities in the scientist's conscience. His moral instinct bore its own justifications and did not have to go through a dialectic analysis; his heart's reasonings were still valid. First, Einstein relied on the myth of progress and had believed that the development of scientific means would suffice to create a cultural and institutional harmony among nations, which would destroy petty nationalism. He abandoned this illusion early enough, however; he considered that it was more efficient to appeal to the people's heart and generosity in order to awaken their conscience. In any case, his antimilitarism was passionate on both esthetical and ethical levels. Military parades, uniforms, *Zusammenmarschieren*, seemed to him to be ridiculous and subhuman. Of the man who submitted himself to that, and said, "He received his brain by mistake; the dorsal spine would have been sufficient."

Only nothing is simple, and moral causes have also their own relativity. Einstein could not have been ignored. Upon returning to his country, after each of his trips around the world, he saw the tottering and cracking of Weimar Germany's liberal facade, the materialization of what he had been the first to denounce — the verbal idealism, hypocrisy and impotence of the League of Nations, and the growth of the Hitlerian monster. He knew that History's tragedies continued to happen on the battlefield of Power. His refusal to accept this situation, that is to say, to play by the rules of the game, resulted in his losing the land who honored the spiritual values in the name of which one has become isolated in purity. When he learned in 1931 that 54% of the American clergy refused on the same principle to participate in any future war, he approved; but in 1933, with Nazi peril so close at hand, he refused to encourage the same kind of objection amongst the Belgian youth who had come to him for advice. And six years later, as a refugee in the United States, at the very moment when the power struggle between racism and democracy broke out, and in agreement with a group of scientists, Albert Einstein wrote his famous letter of August 2, 1939 to Roosevelt. He informed the President of Fermi and Szilard's recent work in the fission of uranium and of the possibility of releasing such destructive power from this fission that one single bomb utilizing it, "exploding in a harbor . . . would destroy the harbor along with the entire surrounding area." He drew the President's attention to the advanced state of German science and research in this field; to the immense danger which threatened the world if one day the Nazis became the first to hold the secret; and to the necessity for the United States to prevent this. Thus the famous Manhattan Project was born — a team of scientists were to work with an enormous budget, to furnish the United States with the A-Bomb, while Hitler, who had had nothing better than the nasty but still primitive little toys, the V2's, had already lost the war and his life.

This story is well-known and has spawned many contradictory reflections. On the one hand, its conclusions are logical; it shows that human events always end up sanctioning stupidity. What could be more ridiculous than the campaign that was launched during the thirties in the Nazi sections of the German universities against "Jewish science" and against Einstein, its most illustrious and therefore most slandered representative? What could be more frenzied in these people who attempted to play remorselessly with power, than the violent purges based on an idiotic philosophy which resulted in putting into the hands of their enemies the Superman who was to discover the decisive power inherent to the atom?

But, on the other hand, the story of the atomic bomb illustrates a cruel paradox: this humane scientist was to bear the responsibility for initiating and extensively collaborating in the creation of a weapon which opened a new era in history, subjecting humanity to the most severe peril and the deepest anguish. Had he thus sinned against humanity, had he failed in his humanist vocation? In any case his own fate became of particular interest, as it presented a broad and serious question to the contemporary mind: that of the relationship between humanism and science. The question has been framed in the abstract; the human drama of Einstein's thought appears therein in its true light and with all of its meaning.

The word humanism has too many meanings, and it is necessary to specify the sense under which it is taken before entering the discussion. Humanism is here perceived as any system of ideas which allows man to have faith in a coherent understanding of his own nature and experience. This understanding can be arrogantly self-centered if man chooses to think of the world only in relation to himself and consider himself as the only measure of things; on the contrary, humanism can also be a reflection of religion, insuring the dignity of man with the help of some reasonable government of divine origin. But there can only be humanism where disbelief and despair are excluded. These can then be abandoned only if the rights and powers of the mind are recognized. Any philosophy which claims to see man only as a superior animal, stands clear of humanism. We must admit that the main element of this superiority is the use of the mind and that human behavior *par excellence* surpasses this essential order with the more spiritual one. Any set of ethics (such as racism, for example) which overemphasizes blood, instinct, and lust for power and force, thereby supressing the superego, and the values belonging to a superior world such as justice, love, and intellectual and esthetic pleasures, also turns its back on humanism. There is even more: any philosophy which identifies the mind solely with intelligence, that is to say as a purely critical and practical faculty, focusing everything on the demands of the body and the extension of material power, such a philosophy which ignores the mind as a source of values, ideals, and aspirations can only father a technological culture, organize the politics of a tyrannical state, and reduce the importance of the wise man and the artist in front of that of the engineer and the commissioner. Once again humanism would be in danger.

If these definitions seem to be correct and conform to what the western conscience has implied by the term humanism (spontaneously at first, and later out of reflection), we see that it expresses the natural ties, but also the real obstacles, in the relationship between humanism and science. At the point of departure, science (insofar as it implies a knowledge of the world) approaches and penetrates the secrets of nature, describes society and explores history; as such it is the substance and instrument of humanism. How could man, himself, be situated in the universe, recognize his own nature and found a morality beyond the simple experience of life, without a methodical inquiry into the immense reality which envelops and sustains him in space and time? In Greek, *Sophia* means both science and wisdom. The philosopher is not always a sage, but he is a man seeking truth, the truth of the world as well as the soul, and consequently he is also partly a scientist. Throughout the history of western culture, metaphysics has been conceived as a final and synthetic view which rests on the very principles of the sciences of nature and life. Man, in order to be happy and strong, needs to understand his domain — the earth and the heavens — and science gives him both the key and the map. Science explains and summarizes. It lights up the past and predicts the future. Since the Renaissance, but especially in the Eighteenth and Nineteenth centuries, Europe nurtured the myth of progress with essentially these two theses: first, that science does necessarily progress (which is true) and that it does continuously improve the well-being, happiness and virtue of humanity (which is less evident).

For half a century now, the acceleration of scientific conquest and the increasing number of technological applications and the elaboration of a civilization prodigiously transformed by the genius of its technicians has profoundly changed the terms of the relationship between humanism and science. Science, in developing man-made expertise at the expense of natural means, and increasing man's power beyond predictable measure, has now outdistanced mankind, and no longer appears humane. Two thousand years ago, the Chinese scholar Chang-Di said that "he who utilizes machines accomplishes mechanically all of his business, carries a mechanical heart in his breast, and loses his pure innocence." This curiously prophetic view, to which Werner Heisenberg* alludes, proved to be only too true. Man saw the dawning of an era of robots, constructed to serve him, but already defying him; and even more seriously, in a society becoming completely manufactured and technocratic, he himself has to fear becoming a robot. What had happened?

First this: science, a purely contemplative activity, detached at its origin, was put to active service (as was natural and probably inevitable) and, like energy which disintegrates as it serves, it lost its original spirituality. For the Ancient Greeks, science was purely an intellectual delight. Only when Syracuse was in the face of danger did the physicist Archimedes agree to construct weapons of war; and Kepler wrote in *Mysterium Cosmographicum*, foreseeing neither the voyages of astronauts nor the trajectories of missiles, "Astronomers satisfy themselves in the simple glory of

---

Nature in Contemporary Physics.

knowing that they have written their works for wise men and not for the swarming crowd, for kings and not for swineherds.'' However, at that time, Leonardo had already dreamt of governing nature with intellectual devices, and Descartes initiated the movement which, through the Encyclopaedists and the Ideologists, would lead to the Marxist idea of a philosophy of *praxis*, action on the world and on history. The scientist and the engineer would become neighbors in the laboratory, and the former would be offering his discoveries to the latter, and occasionally the latter would encourage the first to make finds, up to the day when science and technology would, together in the same domain, have gotten an operative knowledge of the order of facts and events.

Thus the trench was deepened between science and pure rational curiosity in search of truth. Humanism surely lost something, but not everything, for as long as one could still hope that the efficiency pursued by the scientist, the contemplator turned into a manufacturer, would lead to a better life, a better being, and a better way of thinking for the human race. The tragic events of the twentieth century — murderous world wars, massive and anti-liberal revolutions, genocide, totalitarian and concentrationary institutions, have shattered this illusion. Evidence has proven that science immensely increases man's strength but that it guarantees nothing as to whether this strength will be put to good or evil use; the physicists' progress has brought close to nothing in the way of perfecting the moral being. With the ever-widening gap between science and conscience, there is plenty of room for catastrophe to make its way and for the species and even the planet to be endangered; the shock of Hiroshima and the H-bomb's monstrous mushroom clouds in its experimental blasts marked the sky with the sign of the Apocalypse — man was organizing the end of the world himself, without waiting for God's order. An element appeared which would have been unthinkable to Huyghens, Newton, d'Alembert, Condorcet, Faraday, Claude Bernard, Pasteur, or Hertz: fear had entered the laboratories. The scientist suddenly felt responsible for the more than magical powers given to man, and shuddered at the thought of what still might be discovered. One scientist admitted, "Hell can emerge from our equations."

This is the context in which we must situate the great shifting of Einstein's thought after August 6, 1945. We understand the motives which led this idealist, this liberal, and this pacifist to advise and serve in the construction of the first atomic bomb. He accepted the weight of history, he resorted to impure means in order to keep a presumably pure cause out of harm's way; humanist courage can take such detours, crossing the most slippery precipices. But if it was necessary to call on the power of the atom to prevent Hitler and his barbaric racism from triumphing over the world, it didn't follow, in the philosopher-scientist's judgment, that we had the right to use it to put the virtually conquered Japan down to its knees. Yet this happened. Although the course was foreseeable, Einstein witnessed the outcome of the enterprise in which he had played a part with a tortured soul. It was a part that was perhaps less important, less determining, than he thought, but that is of little significance. In the test of moral conscience that he put himself to, his responsibility as an accomplice could not be put in doubt. Then he threw himself into action; he traveled, he spoke, he wrote to awaken the conscience of statesmen and to influence public opinion. His voice mingled with the voices of Oppenheimer and Shapley, who also denounced the enormity of the atomic peril. He adopted the ideas of Emery Reves who recommended, in *Anatomy of Peace*, the establishment of a world government to bring to the individual states a greater knowledge of the secrets of thermonuclear weapons and their use. At that point, one spoke of the naiveté, the loss of a sense of reality which suddenly befell the great scientist. No doubt, if one considers such ideas with an eye towards immediate materialization they do appear to be quite inconsistent, and Einstein's politics seem to be marked by this strangely visionary character which was popular at first but was soon lost in the indifference, if not the kind of irony with which the attempts made by Davis, citizen of the world were received. However one should think about it; if the idea of a world government is irrational, it is so because it does not take into account the irrationality of man. In a time when the progress of science is such that it puts an instrument that has the potential to destroy the species and the planet into the hands of men, then the progress of conscience ought to advance to the point where the universal organization of humanity ceases to be a Utopian concept and appears, on the contrary, as a logical necessity. Einstein only lacked good sense in this affair by having expected more of his contemporaries than they were able to produce.

Moreover, in all his anguish and disappointments, he understood and expressed what was profoundly just with exceptional force; he recognized the catastrophe this suggested to the human personality and the downfall of science in a world where the state is provided with all the power, undertaking and absorbing everything. Here we can refer to the very rich text of his *Message to the Italian Scientists* from 1950 (shortly before his death, Einstein authorized Charles-Noel Martin to reprint this text in his work, *Has H-Hour Sounded for the World?*) which called attention to the biological threat created by the growing number of experimental atomic explosions. The great theorist of General Relativity reassumed his grand stature as the man in the laboratory who seeks nothing more than the truth, which "in more modest terms," he said, "meant a logically constructed comprehension of the world which was accessible through experiment," and he denounced all practical finality in scientific activities. He boldly returned to the aristocratic Greek concept according to which a scientist is a philosopher and not an engineer, refusing to consider himself as a man of science "who has learned to use instruments and adopt work methods which, directly or indirectly only appear scientific, but rather as one in whom the scientific mentality really lives." But, was this necessity of absolute purity in the exploration of nature considered too theoretical and in any case, too unrealistic in the present state of civilization? This time, with a sharp sense of reality, Einstein wrote, "The man of science is conscious of the fact that the application of his research has concentrated first economic, then political power in the hands of a small minority. That is to say that the scientist will be able to hasten, most efficiently, the slide towards a catastrophic state of affairs, "a material submission to the exterior world," an extreme threat for the individual, through the suppression of the mind's freedom. Now no one is more threatened by his own vocation and by nature than the scientist, who needs this freedom more than anything else; and his lot truly becomes "tragic". "Sustained by his aspirations towards clarity and external independence, he himself forges the tools of his exterior enslavement and the annihilation of his personality with his superhuman forces." He furnished the state with instruments of total power, without being able to prevent the fact that they "may lead to total destruction," and "he belittles himself to the point of helping to perfect the means of man's total destruction. Einstein was much less convincing in suggesting possible remedies, a legal one, with a world government, and moral one, with the conversion of scientists to uncompromised, pure science — than when he was when expressing and delineating the horror of this spiritual failure.

Thus Einstein brought to light humanism's divorce from science in a most dramatic way. It was no longer evident that science works for the good of the species and the well-being of the individual; the clever devices that science substitutes for nature, and the unlimited powers that it gives to free agents, allowing them to kill, produce a threat that the physicist with his instruments and equations, can no longer avoid taking into account. Oppenheimer reports that in his last days the old master declared with his typical sense of humor that if he had to start his life all over, he would be a plumber. In a way that is less spectacular, but more dialectic, and no less radical, our century has seen this same rift deepen, no longer in the technological applications of science, but in its main context. Here again, the progress of knowledge has increased human distress; Einstein witnessed this intellectual disease, all the more disturbing to him, because he was one of its instigators.

In order to allow a vision of the world to be humanist, it must include a minimum of optimism, or more precisely, intellectual security. What had prevailed until the time of Copernicus had been very reassuring: a flat and immobile Earth, the center of the Universe, under a sky where fixed stars, constellations, the sun, the moon, the planets all maintained a constant, measurable and predictable relationship in their immobility as well as in their movements. And man emerged on this Earth from a mysterious but presumably recent past, king of a creation made for him. When it appeared that the Earth moved around the Sun, and that the Sun was not even the center of the world, but only one out of the many stars which gravitate in the infinite abyss of the heaven, it came as quite a shock.

Yet Kepler, so dazzled by the order of this creation, felt that by its very immensity, this system that was organized for man did not depart from God's majesty. Moreover, if man has less pride in the place that he sees himself occupying in the universe, the very progress in this type of knowledge increases his confidence in his reason, which is analogous to that of God's. Galileo believed that if human intelligence is infinitely less than God's, still his grasp of mathematical and physical truths is equal. We can't know everything existing in the world but those things which we do understand are true. The development of science through the experimental methods ruling observation, controlling hypotheses and introducing laws, and the power given to nature by the verified regularity and flawless understanding of these laws, re-established man's supremacy in a cosmos where he no longer held his dignity because of a princely election, but because of the genius of a demiurge. At the end of the nineteenth century, the scientific view of the world was a set of coherent mechanics which could be translated by mathematical laws, and the objectivity and constancy of which seemed to be absolutely confirmed by the success of the techniques used in its application. The human mind held a power over things and a mastery of energies that it had never known, at the same time experiencing the intellectual comfort that Ptolemy's system, Aristotle's physics and St. Thomas Aquinas' cosmology had once given to it.

However, from the end of the last century, and especially in the last two-thirds of ours, with the continuous acceleration produced by the incredible extension of discoveries, this handsome balance between humanist confidence and scientific certainty has come to be compromised. Newly explored domains — those of electromagnetic waves, radioactivity and nuclear physics — have risen that no longer submit to the laws of classical physics. De Broglie's wave mechanics do not fit in with the laws of probability, Planck's quantum theory recognizes indeterminate zones in the behavior of atomic particles, and Werner Heisenberg has gone so far as to formulate an "uncertainty principle" in physics. Intellectual categories which had appeared to be clear and distinct, such as time and space, contingency and necessity, efficient cause and final cause, position and speed, energy and extent, mind and matter tend to telescope each other, if not to blend into each other. Even notions where distinctions appeared to be objective and controllable by instruments, like the particle and the wave, come to be employed simultaneously, even by necessity, in elaborating first a theory of light, and then one of matter, on today's level of analysis where we observe phenomena, create hypotheses and invent our experiments. Oppenheimer had to force the mind itself to recognize a "principle of complementarity" which went back to admitting that a thing is other than what it is. The first paradox stated that laws, though they are always statistical, when applied to the global phenomena of macrophysics, nevertheless have a probability equivalent to determinism, signifying that the indetermination of things established in principle has no effect on their development and their relationships. The second paradox lies in the fact that whenever the era when man draws the most precise and spectacular applications from his scientific knowledge comes he finds himself putting the objectivity of science in doubt. As scientists now see things, there is no observation where the observer's point of view does not introduce an element of relativity. As Werner Heisenberg said, "The subject of research is not nature in itself, but rather nature submitted to human interrogation." Thus, the beautiful, solid, structure that science had constructed for man, a structure in which he had constantly known where he stood, what he could do and what was going to happen to him, began collapsing.

There is no doubt that Einstein's theories of General Relativity have been among the most decisive intellectual events which left the modern vision of the universe so confused and uncertain. These theories, very naturally, were projected into non-scientific thought, and affected the philosophy of their time. It is important to note however, that this could not have happened only through the ambiguity of a word. Mathematical relativity is too difficult to grasp for one to understand it when one is not in the field; it is completely different from moral, esthetic, and philosophical relativity. Nevertheless, it is like an indirect confirmation of this philosophy, which had vaguely been recognized by the masses. When Einstein appeared in Paris in the spring of 1922, the latest fad was to criticize dogmatic rationalism; Bergson still enjoyed great prestige, literary impressionism triumphed with Paul Morand, dilettantism with Cocteau, irrationalism with the young people who dabbled in Dada and prepared to organize a more dangerous machine called surrealism, in order to disrupt manners and ideas. All this was far from Einstein, but the idea that relativity was the last word in science was not without pleasing the literati, or fitting the moral of the day since society was then wavering between corrupted memories of a horrible and absurd war and the euphoria of recovered peace. A woman could say to a lover who still spoke romantically of absolute love, "But my dear, the absolute? haven't you read Einstein?" It was rather foolish, but not much more than the pedantic reasoning of the Nazi theorists who, starting from the fact that the triumph of democracy is linked to scientific materialism, sought at first to employ relativity in order to support a political revolution that they claimed was based on German Idealism; thus spoke Goebbels and Jordan. Soon others covered these early declarations, for, when they learned that Einstein was not Aryan, they denounced the eternal destruction and anarchistic ferment of Jewish thought present in this philosophy. Marxists also accused him of attracting the youth to bourgeois idealism; certain theologians found an unpleasant taste of atheist materialism in the theory of General Relativity, while others tried to use it as an emergency measure to fight mechanism and determinism.

These speculations, these extrapolations, were of a pretty low level. The honest choice would have been to ask Einstein himself what were the philosophical consequences that he drew from his theory. It is a delicate question, for which we can only give a general answer.

In fact, it seems that there was, if not a logical contradiction, at least a dialectic tension in Einstein's thought: we can, in effect, either draw subjective sense from it, one which makes science a creation of the mind, or a dogmatic sense, asserted absolutely as it sees knowledge in mathematical translations. There is no doubt that relativity implies, at least at its point of departure, a certain skepticism proper to devaluating scientific definitions. In the critical observation, this skepticism stems out of the subjectivity of the observer, the arbitrary choice of experiments, as well as of the instruments used tends to give a subjective quality to science. Through other paths Einstein here comes close to Henri Poincaré's thought, enlarging the creative role of the imagination which invents the hypotheses in the formulation of general laws. On the other hand, Einstein's careful positivist attitude inclined him, as much before the facts of the physical world as of the moral, to accept complexity and contingency while maintaining all logical and doctrinal systematization. This open state of mind, this certain welcoming spirit which was necessary to any disciplined research, but which he himself cultivated with special care and which no doubt remained at the base of his original discoveries concerning the nature of light and matter, made him into the opposite of a dogmatist and tended to help him imagine an idea of the cosmos that conformed carefully to its established complexity.

However, nothing would be more incorrect than denying Einstein's general idea of a synthesis, but also his intention of finding it. In defining the goal of scientific research to Italian scientists — that is, a will to acquire knowledge, not only consider its practical usage — he wrote: "It is in the nature of this aspiration, to tend to dominate all the diverse and multiple aspects of experiments, and to tend towards a

simplification and limitation of basic hypotheses,'': a
simplification and limitation which was only perfectly attained with the mathematical formulation of the law. On this
fundamental point Einstein appears more to be the faithful
heir than the mystic destroyer of what the ambition of
humanist science had been since the Renaissance and particularly in the nineteenth century: to arrive at a mathematical expression translating nature. To come to that he never
put the human faculties in doubt nor the methods of his
culture, and furthermore he guarded himself from conclud-
ing, as many hurried minds often do, that the instrument of
knowledge would be overthrown by the expansion of their
same knowledge. His famous remark is often quoted, ''The
most incomprehensible thing in the world is that the world is
comprehendible,'' which is the most beautiful flattery ever
accorded to the human intellect.

Following his own way of thinking, he was rather of-
fended by the experiments of his followers and disciples
revealing important areas of indeterminability in the mi-
crophysical domain. He fought Planck and Bohr, admitting
that the established anamolies should one day be interpreted
in an expanded theory where the fundamental notions of
classical physics would recover their value. ''Einstein,''
wrote Robert Oppenheimer,* ''was reduced to declaring
that quantum theory didn't please him. He didn't like the
elements of indeterminism that it contained. He refused to
renounce causality, continuity. He had lived with these notions, he had once rescued them by expanding them, and
then he saw them lost; even if he himself had put the dagger
in the murderer's hands, this loss made his work painful for
him.'' He reassured himself by inventing picturesque formulas which often showed a great depth of thought: ''God,''
he said, ''is complicated, but he surely isn't mean.'' By this

---

*Speech to UNESCO. *Le Nouvel Observateur,* December, 1965.

we understand that Einstein, like Descartes, shook off the hypothesis of an evil genius who would put the universe in absolute disorder, irreducible by law and superior reason. He also added: "I can't believe that God plays dice with the world," meaning that he opted for a rational intention in a cosmos which cannot surrender to the domination of contingency. Thus the theorist of relativity sought to reassure himself in a world where he didn't want to find the human intelligence battered and despaired by the complexity of things, neither in the infinite entanglements of the galaxies nor in the caprice of the atoms.

On December 15, 1965 a ceremony at the Unesco brought together the greatest living scientists of the time — Louis de Broglie, Robert Oppenheimer, Julian Huxley, to celebrate the tenth anniversary of Einstein's death. Because the forward motion of science does not stop and because the honor of men of science never allows them to lie, even in their praise, the position of a theorist of relativity and the famous equation of the equality of mass and energy were described objectively by his peers, who recognized both the creative originality and the fruitful role of his thought, as well as the weakness or loss of validity of some of his theories, such as the experiments and the further analysis of his disciples brings them out today. At the level of rational or speculative constructions of these extraordinary minds, the verification of an error or an illusion by one of them doesn't imply any reprobation, nor loss of esteem on the part of the others, since the progress of science is made, at constant risk, by the art of the creative imagination which brings forward an hypothesis and waits for sanction of experimentation. But one thing was understood: the sincerity of the homage paid to the man named Albert Einstein was unanimous. A scientist can have been a disembodied intellect, an exceptionally well organized and dynamic brain, functioning in the manner of a computer in order to logically draw an enormous amount of data, classed and fixed by the memory, an explicative result, inspiringly simple, which is precise conquest of science. Such a prodigy is to man's honor, but does not engage all of the man. Einstein's scientific personality came to this point and surpassed it; and considering the best out of him, he was of another type. With him the line was not cut between the soul and the intellect, between science and conscience; a superman by the strength of his cerebral organization, he remained in thought and feeling a man among men, linked to them by responsibility and friendship, bearing their problems with him, clearing these problems for them and looking for the answers. Through the most abstract speculation, he crossed two great thresholds; the metaphysical imagination which allows a sensible notion of the universe to surface, and the love for humanity which encourages one to lead a better life on earth. At this double title, he deserves to be called a humanist scientist.

CHAPTER SEVEN

The Philosopher-Scientist

by FRANÇOIS RUSSO

Albert Einstein Philosopher-Scientist. That is the title of the work offered to Einstein in 1949, celebrating his seventieth birthday. In this book we find a series of remarkable studies on the philosophical aspects of his accomplishments. The completion of such a work justifies our taking the opportunity here to reflect on Einstein's thought and contribution. These reflections are, for the greater part, based on these earlier essays, two of which Einstein actually wrote himself.

To what degree and from which point of view can Einstein be considered as a philosopher? In order to answer, one has to place oneself in a rather broad perspective, expanding beyond the traditional boundaries of philosophy as they are understood in a strict sense, and follow this declaration from Einstein's autobiography: "The essential thing in the existence of a man like me resides in what he thinks and the manner in which he thinks" (*was er denkt und wie er denkt*) — Einstein himself underlined this "and not in what he does and suffers."

Einstein was not a true philosopher in the "professional" sense. He didn't really leave us an elaborate and systematic doctrine of knowledge, nor of metaphysics nor cosmology. From this point of view Einstein was less a philosopher than his contemporaries, Duhem and Poincaré, who not only proposed explicit doctrines of science, but also defended them more than he did.

However if one goes beyond this somewhat formal and strict conception of the function of philosophy and looks for an essential reflection of the nature and the meaning of things, then Einstein (at least in what concerns the physical world) becomes a philosopher in the most authentic sense of the word: At the basis of his own reasonings, one finds an unremitting interest in understanding the physical world, and reaching its final causes. This had nothing to do with any detached and autonomous speculation, his was a reflection which matured through the progression of his scientific experiments. From this point of view Albert Einstein was much more a philosopher than Pierre Duhem and Henri Poincaré, whose philosophy seems to have been superimposed over their scientific attitudes, and to come from independents, more from *a priori* views than from the "experience" of science.

More precisely Einstein is seen as a philosopher, and as a true philosopher of science because he was always conscious of his intellectual progression and of its consequences, and he took great care in justifying them all. He made his steps explicit in very clear and often solemn declarations; he even fought to defend his "epistemology," notably in a famous discussion with Bohr in 1935 (which we will give an account of later on) and in the last chapter, "Response to Criticisms," which was comprised in the anniversary publication mentioned earlier.

While Einstein also chose to be a philosopher because of the nature of his mind, he did so mainly by necessity. Circumstances were such that he found himself at a moment in the development of science where the essential task to be accomplished was a philosophical one. What physics absolutely needed at the beginning of the twentieth century was a critical reflection on its principles, a questioning of its basic notions and, in all regards, of scientific method itself. More than any other contemporary physicist, Einstein perceived this necessity and set himself to the task of answering it. In this way, Einstein was a philosopher in action, he felt committed. This is what gives his philosophy such worth, and superiority over other philosophies of science; those are no doubt valuable but much more conceptual, verbal, and more *a priori*. This is why Einstein's philosophy was sometimes called, in fact, even by himself, "opportunist." Einstein — and more of this will be discussed later — was at the same time a positivist, a realist, and an idealist. He refused to allow himself to be enclosed in a unilateral concept of knowledge, no doubt more pure, more "philosophical," and easier to explain, but finally not truly legitimate or fully adjusted to the mind's progression, one which was also occasionally sterilizing in regard to the service of science.

For all this, one mustn't believe that Einstein's thought developed in ignorance of philosophy. No doubt Einstein had only a limited knowledge of the great philosophers; nevertheless he was familiar with a fairly large number of them. Thus, more particularly, he had read Kant and Hume, declaring that he owed much to them. But their lessons had been like a dead language; they could not be of any use to the progress of science without Einstein's very personal endeavors as he understood and corrected their views in order to adapt them to the very precise situations which he was facing. In the presence of such a philosophic attitude in a scientist, one understands why a philosophy which is detached from scientific experimentation, such as those which belong to the past but which one occasionally encounters today, is of such little value, and even becomes a subject of caution at least in the field of non-human realities. Einstein was less preoccupied with defining modes of thinking and presenting a general epistemology, than with finding the attitude of mind most capable of perceiving the solutions of problems. Thus he became a positivist — we will return to this point a little later — in order to deny the simultaneity of events which are detached from one another. But in reality, because of the importance of the questions that he treated and because of the penetration of this thought, he was one of those directly responsible for defining the modes of scientific thought with greater precision. He is seen as one of the principal "inventors" of the modern scientific method, which was still so imprecise at the end of the nineteenth century, in spite of the assurance of those who were promoting it. Thus, we owe the right definition of the positivist attitude to Einstein, as well as a much larger and deeper perception of the possibilities one has of understanding phenomena.

Outside of its explicit or live manifestation, the philosophical significance of Einstein's thought and work is also attested by the philosophers who paid attention to his work. The philosophical speculations which gave way to Einstein's discoveries are rich in information. But we don't know whether, in the end, their evaluation is a positive one. For in spite of the efforts of some great minds, Einstein's reflections are at the origin. Prehensibility hasn't yielded, even to the efforts of so many misunderstandings and incomprehensions. We know how much Bergson rebelled against Relativity, unable to accept the denial of the absolute character of time. And Merleau-Ponty manifested a very summary, and even yet from certain points of view, erroneous interpretations of Einstein's ideas in his classes at the Collège de France. Moreover, even though it has now been accepted, Einstein's "philosophy" — principally his views on space and time — is often understood in an overly scholarly and impoverished manner. We remember its more simple aspects, those which are at the periphery of his reflection without understanding the profound dynamism which animated his thinking. Or else we take into consideration the most disputed aspects of his thought, notably the great unifying views he professed at the end of his life, and which are far from having the quality and importance of his work of 1905 (the Restricted Theory of Relativity) or 1915 (the theory of General Relativity).

No doubt Einstein's principal contribution to philosophy resides in the fact that he obliged philosophers to recognize the fragility and incompleteness of the considerations that they had held as indisputable and under the "shelter" of scientific development. This is precisely what happened with the notions of space and time, which had been burdened with common traditional views and Kantian dogmatism. The notion of space had already, in the course of the nineteenth century, been shaken by non-Euclidean geometry. It was even pushed further aside when Einstein demonstrated, with the discovery of General Relativity, that space isn't an inert framework for physical phenomena. As for the notion of time, as we have just said, philosophers were profoundly disturbed by its relativization. They didn't entirely accept it — perhaps with reason. They maintained that, aside from physical time such as Einstein defined it, there is room for a notion of time which is, in a certain manner, independent, by the fact that it refers to living experience. But, even in introducing this distinction, philosophers had to agree that they were submitting more and more to the control of science. They understood that they had to take science more into account than they had thought.

From then on, philosophy came to appear less predominant, less autonomous than had been believed up to that time.

If we define the positivist attitude as a submission to facts, it certainly constitutes the major characteristic of Einstein's scientific progression. But, in a larger framework of this definition, many different forms of positivism may take place. Also, when one discusses Einstein's positivism, one should carefully and precisely define its nature, because otherwise one runs the risk of making some truly equivocal statements. Furthermore, one can notice a certain evolution in his career as a positivist, in the way that he gave more and more recognition to the role played by the activity of the mind in scientific knowledge.

Along with all positivists, Einstein held that only the notions which could effectively be elaborated from experimentation and which, could in reverse be submitted to the physicist's control, were acceptable. It was because the time and space of classical physics did not meet with these standards that Einstein rejected them.

Thus understood, positivism appears to constitute an essential condition to the development of science. Modern science owes a great part of its success to the rejection of the "philosopher's," *a priori* notions. From 1921 on, Einstein was very clear in his explanations on this subject: "The only justifications of our concepts is that they serve to represent the complexity of our experiments. Outside of that, they are not legitimate. I am convinced that philosophers have had a detrimental influence on the progress of scientific thought by taking certain fundamental concepts away from the domain of empiricism, where they were subjected to a given control, in order to place them in the inaccessible heights of *a priori*." (From *The Meaning of Relativity*.)

Criticizing the notions of time and simultaneity, Einstein declared even more explicitly in the *Theory of Relativity*: "The notion of simultaneity only exists for the physicist if he has discovered the possibility of determining that two events are simultaneous in practice. As long as this condition is not filled physicists are wrong — and probably non-physicists also — to imagine that they are able to give a sense of simultaneity to two phenomena."

But, with certain scientists and philosophers of science, a second side is added to the positivism that we have just defined: the refusal to recognize any other physical reality than what is immediately offered by the experiment, and the repudiation of the mind's creative role in the constitution of science. Einstein never wanted to see this kind of positivism; he even vigorously opposed it. To him the claim that one could thus restrict the mind's dynamism in an effort to understand the physical world was simply inadmissible. For him, the fact that the mind was free to create was essential to science. He even insisted on this point so much that several of those who interpreted his thought came to minimize the role of the positivist attitude in his discoveries, particularly the ones dating from 1905, from which the theory of Restricted Relativity was issued. Some have even gone so far as to say that Einstein had progressively abandoned positivism. When it was observed, after his debates with Bohr over quantum mechanics, that by refusing the indeterminist point of view he was not being faithful to the positivism of his youth, he had this response, "A good joke shouldn't be repeated too often." But this does not totally reflect Einstein's attitude. If he had been led to give still a greater importance to the creations of the mind, he, however, never rejected the basic rules of positivism which he had established in his first great works.

Therefore, before describing the most rational aspects of Einstein's attitude, it will be useful to define the nature and range of his positivism a little more precisely.

One might think that, while adopting a positivist attitude, principally in the criticism of the notions of space and time and also, in a more subtle and perhaps even deeper fashion, in the criticism of the measurement of distance which contributed to the introduction of curved space in General Relativity, Einstein was only following a traditional method and that, in this regard, his merit is not great. This analysis presents a rather imprecise view of the conditions under which Einstein introduced these new notions.

No doubt, the positivist ideal had deeply influenced the concepts of science at the beginning of the twentieth century. But it cannot be overemphasized that it was in fact not much used in actual practice. At least it hadn't been pushed to its very limit. Priority had been given to facts and observation, and a certain number of *a priori* concepts had been rejected, but one had not taken the care to submit all the notions existing in science to the test of the positivist rules. On the other hand, in order to put positivism to work, it wasn't enough to condemn the notions and theories which didn't yield to it; it was actually necessary to construct a positivist science. This task wasn't easy.

Einstein's great merit — we might say his glory — precisely consisted in fully evaluating all these requirements and boldly deciding to meet them.

Because he assumed this task in an original and personal manner, it is necessary to recognize that he had been directly encouraged by certain philosophers who, better than others, had already found how to precisely and penetratingly define what a truly positivist attitude ought to be, notably Ernst Mach, professor at the University of Vienna, and a scientist and a philosopher at the same time. Einstein declared in his autobiography that Mach's philosophical writings, as well as Hume's, although in a less direct manner, had played a decisive role (*eintscheidend*) in the initial effort that led to the reformation of the notions of time and space.

We cannot admire Einstein's audacity and resolution enough, for he showed so much of it in rejecting the notions of time, simultaneity at a distance, and absolute space, notions which had been so deeply anchored in the mind of man. The mind clung so tenaciously to these notions that Poincaré hadn't dared to broach this step, even though he, like Einstein, had recognized that these traditional ideas couldn't be made to agree with positivist science.

It is also necessary to underline how it seemed contrary to the spontaneous attitude of the mind to stop, at least momentarily, looking for the how and why of things (here the nature of time and space), in order to consider them as only being definable through a series of rather down to earth observations. Against all predictions, this attitude revealed itself as being extraordinarily productive. Undoubtedly, the Einsteinian revolution also supposed an inductive power and a profound perception of the nature of the physical world; and one should not forget that, without this radically positivist method, it would never have happened.

It is necessary to explain precisely what are the place and significance of positivism in Einstein's work. But, as we have already indicated, it is also necessary — once again — to underline his confidence in the power of reason which also animated his work. In 1905, with the discovery of Special Relativity, Einstein stayed close to the facts, while developing an already remarkable rational construction. But, a little later when he introduced a quadridimensional notion of the space-time concept, with the help of Minowski, and especially afterwards when he founded the theory of General Relativity, he had to engage in speculation that was going to put the immediate data of experiment singularly at a distance, leading him little by little into recognizing that the mind was capable of reconstructing the world, and that the world was rational. It was a situation which provoked his astonishment and which he expressed in the famous formula already cited in the preceding chapter: "The most incomprehensible thing in the world is that the world is comprehensible."

This faith in the power of reason came to constitute the essence of what he called his "epistemological credo." He himself told us in his autobiography, written in 1948, that this belief developed slowly; it did not correspond to the position he took in his youth. At that time (as said earlier) he closely followed Mach's positivist doctrine. But, he stated, "that position appears untenable to me today. It doesn't give enough room to the essentially constructive and speculative nature of thought and, more especially, of scientific thought." Already in 1916, he had opposed the doctrine upheld by Mach, according to which the task of science uniquely consisted in organizing ones own observations, while general laws were only an economic means of retaining individual facts.

Nor would Einstein admit that the role of reason in science should be limited to pure logical deductions. For him, science was in its fundamental movement essentially a creative act of the mind.

He explained himself even more completely on this subject at a 1933 conference in London: "Philosophers of Nature", in the eighteenth and nineteenth centuries, were for the most part dominated by the idea that the fundamental concepts and postulates of physics were not in the logical sense free creations of the human mind, but had to be deduced by "abstractions," that is to say by logical means. A clear recognition of the falseness of this concept has been furnished by the theory of General Relativity. We cannot hope to deduce its basic concepts and postulates in a logical way."

This confidence in the power of reason even led Einstein to declare that "in a certain sense (he) held as true that pure thinking could reach reality, as the Ancients did."

As early as in 1905, although he was then still close to positivism, Einstein had committed himself to free creation, in that year however, through a profound induction which carried him way beyond the immediate data of the senses and the usual modes of thinking, he established the principles of Special Relativity. Numerous experimented verifications came soon enough to justify his audacity. But we know that it wasn't going to be the same afterwards with the General

Theory of Relativity, for its verifications were, in Einstein's life, rare and contested. This time it was especially the confidence that he had in the validity of his intellectual steps which sustained his belief in the truth of his theory.

Drawing the lesson himself from the conditions through which his discoveries had been obtained, Einstein made this remark, which had very broad implications: "the distance in thought between fundamental concepts and laws on one side and, on the other, the conclusions that we draw from the experiment becomes greater and greater." It seems that, before Einstein, the human mind had never established a valid scientific doctrine which was so detached from experimental data. His doctrine is so far from the ambitious constructions in physics of the past centuries: Aristotle's four elements, Descartes vortices, Boscovich's attractions . . . Theories where one certainly encountered profound views, but which were laden with imaginary, puerile reasonings. Einsteinian construction is all of another style: only the notions which can be entirely reconstructed by the mind are accepted and, as audacious as the hypotheses at the basis of his theories are, their development is submitted to a strict rational control, and the pitiless requirements of coherence.

Also, though Einstein saw the fear of metaphysics manifested by contemporary empiricists as a veritable illness of the mind, it was absolutely not, for him, a way of praising a return towards the easy, imaginative and sentimental metaphysics, but, on the contrary, very different constructions, essentially founded on an adult rationality which was able to assess the real possibilities of the mind.

Naturally one could think that it was above all the very broad use that Einstein made of mathematics which showed him taste for rational constructions. And many are those who in fact measure their esteem for Einstein in the complexity and high level of his mathematical developments. But such a view doesn't correspond to reality and may even lead to a false appreciation of Einstein's merit. If it is true that the mathematical instrument holds an important place in Einstein's work, it wasn't in its use that Einstein gave the greatest proof of his originality and of his creative power. It is much more in his fundamental reflection on the basic notions of physics, the explanation of which cover very few pages, and only employs very simple mathematics.

It was only rather late that Einstein got effectively preoccupied with mathematics. He bent himself to their austere abstraction, understanding that it was necessary for the development of his ideas. "When I was a student," he tells us in his autobiography, "it didn't seem clear to me that the most fundamental concepts in physics were linked to the finest mathematical methods. This only became obvious to me after years of personal work."

Actually, the 1905 treatise which founded Special Relativity rests but little on mathematics. In 1908, Einstein introduced quadridimensional space-time, but it was especially in the following years that, in order to establish the theory of General Relativity, Einstein was led to make a great deal more use of highly sophisticated mathematics. But he did not create the mathematics that were necessary to him; he found them in the arsenal of existing mathematics: in Riemann's curved space, conceived in the nineteenth century, and especially in the absolute differential calculus from the Italians Civita and Ricci — the latter's fundamental treatise dating from 1900. When, later, he needed more complex spaces, it was the French mathematician Elie Cartan who furnished them.

Einstein's essential creative steps are encountered less in his mathematical elaborations than in his "experiments in thought." By this specific expression one should understand a chain of deductions and inductions that stem from a penetrating and rigorous logical analysis of experimental situations. It was through these steps that Einstein was led, in 1905, to establish the principle of the constancy of the speed of light, to reject the notion of absolute time and, later, between 1908 and 1915, to identify inertia and gravitation. It is the energy and lucidity with which he led this reflection, the intellectual courage that he showed in refusing to allow himself to be affected by the habits of the mind which are traditional but not founded in reason, that should be recognized as his greatest merit. No doubt these basic views led to new mathematical developments; these allowed him to strengthen his concepts and to draw most important consequences from them, some of which were completely unsuspected. But the essence of Einstein's creative effort doesn't reside in his mathematical methods.

"Physics is an attempt to grasp what exists as something comprehensible which can be thought independently from what we perceive. It is in this sense that we can speak of physical reality." By this definition, which he gave us in his autobiography, Einstein expressed one of the most fundamental views of his conception of science. At the same time it extends and gives full significance to his faith in reason.

In thus asserting that physics can and should attain reality, Einstein not only opposed the positivism which doesn't wish to recognize any realities other than known facts, nor the notions and laws that we can immediately deduce from them, but also the conventionalism of a Poincaré, and a formalism which, despite it recognized the necessity in science to use abstract theories which were separated from the experiment, did not wish to recognize these theories as having a reality.

This realistic aim, Einstein's driving force, was powerfully sustained in the elaboration of relativity, but it was also at the origin of the conflict that opposed him to Bohr, as explained further on.

This is not at all a realism of "things"; Einstein never accepted the unanalyzed entities which are only imaginations or the more or less schematized objectification of sensible experience. His realism (what we have called his faith in reason shows it clearly) was, to use Bachelard's expression, a rational realism. The realities of science are constructed and controlled by the mind, but they are not for the matter arbitrary constructions. They truly express the state of things, or at least they try to reach being through a method of approximation.

More profoundly, the realities that Einstein considered have a consistency, a stability, an essential character that isn't offered by the changing and disordered world of appearances attained by the immediate observation of phenomena.

It was not easy to execute such a project. Often enough, in the past, science believed itself capable of attaining such objective realities. Actually, this rarely came about. What it believed to be a permanent reality, existing independently of the conditions of observation, often turned out to be a poorly defined reality, charged with subjective elements. But, in this pursuit of objectivity, this "search for the absolute" which we encounter all through the history of science. Einstein played a decisive role. Already in Aristotle, and much more explicitly in Descartes, Galileo and especially Newton, this problem had been encountered. But, in the singular field of mechanics, they did not reach a coherent doctrine, asserting the existence of an absolute space and the "indifference" of mechanical laws at the same time, in relation to trihedral figures of rectilinear and uniform movement. By a critical analysis of the fundamental notions of physics, Einstein was not only able to resolve these contradictions, but also those which had resulted from the failure of Michelson's experiment. Through a paradox which moreover was only apparent, in relativizing the notions of space, time and mass (which until then had been considered absolute), Einstein was able to define truly objective realities, in the sense that they are independent of the trihedral figure in relation to which the observations are made. But these new realities are found to be mathematical realities far separated from the sensible. It was only at the price of the mathematization of physics and very abstract constructions that Einstein was able to come to the most essential and most solid facts in physics.

At the same moment that Einstein, at the apex of his career, witnessed the recognition of his discoveries and of all their consequences, the birth of quantum mechanics was introducing profoundly new views, questioning the objectivity of scientific knowledge which, as we said, constituted a fundamental element of Einstein's epistemological beliefs. Between 1927 and 1930, in the memorable meetings where the principles and interpretation of quantum mechanics were discussed, Einstein declared his opposition to the new doctrine. In 1935 he explained it in a very explicit manner in an article, published in *Physical Review*, titled "Can the Description of Physical Reality by Quantum Mechanics Be Considered As Complete?" Bohr replied in the same review in the same year. The debate was taken up again on the occasion of the publication of the anniversary volume which was offered to Einstein in 1949 on his seventieth birthday. Bohr stated his position anew, and, in the book's conclusion, entitled "Response to Criticisms," Einstein confirmed his opinion still more readily.

Science has rarely known a debate more serious and more fundamental. And the adversaries who confronted each other were of the same stature. On the one side Einstein, standing with his major discoveries which had renewed physics and furthermore leaned on the new mechanics; on the other, Bohr and a group of physicists of first rank —

among others, Heisenberg — who had not been superficial in elaborating their doctrine, but considered that it proceeded forthrightly from the same logic of quantum mechanics.

Where was the essential difference? In Einstein's rejection of three principles, narrowly connected, which constitute the basis of the new epistemology:

— quantum physics has the correct description of observation as its only goal;

— physical reality independent of the observer does not exist;

— a more detailed analysis of phenomena than that which is offered by quantum mechanics is excluded by principle and not by conceptual or experimental insufficiency.

What we have previously said regarding Einstein's concept of physical reality and its objectivity allows us to understand to which point these new principles were deeply disturbing to him. He saw in them an "undefendable positivist attitude" which went back to declaring with Berkeley that being is reduced to perceiving: *esse est percipi*.

Certainly Einstein recognized that it was "logically possible to assert without contradiction that quantum mechanics furnishes an exhaustive description of phenomena," but this concept, he declared, "is so contrary to my scientific instinct that I cannot abandon the search for a more complete system of concepts." More precisely Einstein didn't want to admit that one could say that it isn't possible to describe individual situations and that such situations do not have a real existence independent of observation.

Einstein never wanted to renounce the idea that a reality exists, even if no one is there to observe it.

Einstein always considered that quantum mechanics doesn't furnish a complete description of reality and that it should be possible to develop a more adequate representation of phenomena. We know that he wasn't the only one to think so and that even now some authoritative physicists, among them Louis de Broglie, share this conviction. But it is necessary to recognize that, until now, this project hasn't yielded a truly satisfying theory. The most recent interpreters of quantum mechanics have demonstrated that we find ourselves in the presence of a situation essentially characterized by the fact that the individual states which our imagination and classical views believed to be separable, do not seem to be able to be effectively separated, and this is not simply true for experimental reason but also for reasons which appear to proceed from the most profound nature of things.

So one can wonder if one is not today in a situation similar to the one Einstein had to confront in 1905. We are obliged not only to question the fundamental notions of physics, but also our manner of thinking. In the face of quantum mechanics Einstein perhaps didn't have the intellectual courage which had allowed him, in his youth, to surmount the concepts and habits of mind then considered as indisputable, not only by the standards of common knowledge but also by physicists. It was Bohr and his disciples who had the courage this time. Perhaps it was with reason that Bohr was able to respond to Einstein, who was expressing the uncomfortable feeling that he experienced before the apparent failure of certain established principles explaining nature and on which there could be general agreement: "In the task which consists of putting some order into the domain of entirely new experiments, it is hardly possible to have confidence in principles anchored by habit, whatever they are and whatever their generality is; one single necessity still exists, and that is to avoid logical inconsistencies. Now we can say that, in this relation, the formalism of quantum mechanics is entirely satisfying."

No doubt the pursuit of unity, through the essential principles of physical phenomena, constitutes the major characteristic of Einstein's genius. This attraction, this taste, is at
the basis of his greatest discoveries. There he places himself
in line with Kepler, Descartes, Galileo, Newton and Leibniz. But, even more than these, he aimed at a total synthesis
of physical phenomena and, better "equipped" than they
were, he wasn't misled by artificial connections and the
falsely simple notions characteristic of the work of his predecessors, which in their case, confused seriously unifying
views with many imaginary elucubrations. However, as
coherent and comprehensive as Einstein's work is, it doesn't
represent an entirely satisfying synthesis, especially because
it couldn't integrate quantum mechanics. It nonetheless
constitutes the fundamental framework of all modern
physics.

Einstein expressed this ideal of unity himself in one of the
most beautiful pages of his autobiography, which is worth
quoting: "When I approached physics it was split up into
special fields, each of which could absorb an entire life of
work without being able to satisfy one's appetite for the
profound knowledge of things. I found myself in the presence of an overwhelming mass of data of observation and of
very insufficiently coordinated experiments. But I soon
learned the means of attaining the most fundamental realities
by putting off the thousand other things which filled the mind
but which diverted one from the essential." Thus Einstein
states his most fundamental intention, which has less to do
with the discovery of new laws than with formulating, from
the diversity of disciplines and the phenomena, a simple and
most profound doctrine which gave them order and unity.
He expressed himself even more explicitly in the elementary
presentation of Special Relativity that he published in 1921:
"The theory of Special Relativity is derived directly from
electrodynamics and optics. It modifies the assertions of

these sciences very little, but it has considerably simplified the theoretical constructions, which is incomparably more important.''

What he wants to establish is a theory which, inspired by the already ample synthesis that was already shown in the thermodynamics developed in the course of the nineteenth century, can explain a great diversity of phenomena with the help of a small number of principles. ''A theory has all the more reason of being retained,'' he stated again in his autobiography, ''if it shows premises connecting a great number of different things which are the simplest possible, and a field of application which is as extensive as possible. Under this point of view, classical thermodynamics has made a profound impression on me.'' He could also bring up Maxwell's synthesis.

Einstein's synthesis is not to be discussed here; it has been presented in other chapters of this book. But it appears opportune to recall the connections that Einstein was to make between themes and notions until then unrelated, because it was principally this way that he progressively unified physics. Thus in 1905 he established the equivalence of mass and energy and, from 1908 on, of inertia and gravity. While he was at the same time led to relate space to time, he also established profound links between mechanics and electromagnetism, which had been completely unsuspected until then. More audaciously still, in founding the theory of General Relativity, he made translated mechanics into geometrix, demonstrating that the gravitational field ought to be considered as a geometric property of space, mathematically defined as a curve, for space is only without curvature, that is to say Euclidian, in the absence of gravity. This curvature is caused by the presence of matter and it can be calculated from the knowledge of the distribution of matter in space. Guided by this mathematical formalism, but at the price of a bold induction, Einstein established as a principle — which

experimentation would later verify — that a body subjected
to a gravitational field crosses a geodesically curved space,
that is to say, align such as the one constituting the shortest
path between two points.

From the cosmological point of view, this identification
of gravity with the curvature of space undoubtedly constitutes the idea that most profoundly modified the traditional
conception of the physical world. In General Relativity,
space no longer appears as an inert container, indifferent to
its contents, as had still been the case in Special Relativity,
but it was established as having a structure and, therefore, as
possessing also physical properties.

Therefore the primary entities of the physical world —
space, time, matter, energy, the speed of light — are no
longer strangers to one another, as in the classical theories;
they appear intimately related. This unification is nevertheless incomplete in several regards. Einstein was conscious
enough of this. On the one hand, matter and forces of gravity
are no doubt linked by equations, but they don't exist less for
their matter as distinct entities. Einstein's attempts, at the
end of his life, to reduce this plurality were not fully crowned
with success. On the other hand, electrical and magnetic
phenomena do not have a place in this first synthesis. No
doubt Einstein himself, and several other eminent theorists,
including Eddington, have imagined spaces more complex
than curved space in order to extend this geometric representation of phenomena to other than that which is created
in the gravitational field, principally to electromagnetic
phenomena. But these very formal theories finally appear
rather arbitrary and even a little sterile. More seriously,
because it does not integrate quantum mechanics, the
Einsteinian synthesis presents itself not only as an insufficiently refined view of the world, but also as a doctrine which
probably allows a profound aspect of the nature of things to
escape.

As far as it concerns the global comprehension of the physical universe, Einstein had very profound views, notably on the subject of its dimension and on the manner in which matter is distributed. But there also, his theories cannot be considered as entirely satisfying. Moreover, this problem calls for mathematical work whose necessity he recognized in his last years but which he wasn't able to develop himself.

Ten years after his death, in spite of remarkable theoretical developments done by theorists which are better formed and better equipped mathematically than he was, we cannot consider that we hold a true "universal equation" accounting for the totality of physical phenomena. There is only a hope for it, an intention, contrary to what the general public believes, for it is often abused by unscrupulous vulgarizers.

It was an admirable adventure, that this small employee of the Bern patent office who, "starting out on such a good foot," founded, in 1905, at the age of twenty-six, Special Relativity and, ten years later, General Relativity! We cannot fail to see in the quality of this work and of the intellectual effort which is at its origin, as well as in the fundamental questions which rose from it, the most profound revolution of scientific thought in modern times, which highly deserves the philosopher's attention and interest. We have attempted here to discuss its nature and significance, helped by Einstein himself who, better that most of the great scientists, knew how to "reflect" on his own work and on his steps with a great faithfulness in regard to the scientific experience that he was living through. So it was in all truth and justice that we, just as the editor of the anniversary volume, have joined the name of philosopher to his qualifications as a scientist.

CHAPTER EIGHT

Such As We Knew Him

by HILAIRE CUNY

It was 1922 and I was ten years old. I remember a railway station with trains whistling, wagons bumping against each other, and a thousand other noises that would let even a blindfolded person know that he was on the platform of a train station. Nearby, very close to the place where I was standing with my parents, on the side where the suburban lines arrive, an unusual group came into view: very serious gentlemen who seemed to be in a hurry, dressed in the frock coats that we were beginning to make fun of in those days, and in the middle of them was a man who clearly stood out — not that he was taller or bigger than average or that he was behaving differently, but at first glance, because he was bare-headed, a kind of absurdity at the time, and especially because his eyes wandered, with a kind of amused irony, over his entourage and his surroundings. For an instant his eyes met mine for a very little time, but staring all the same, and then they went back to examining the crowd and everything around.

Albert Einstein had come, almost clandestinely, to France, although he received a very official invitation. The hatred for Germany was still very strong, in spite of the victory and, at the insistence of several members of the

Academy of Sciences, who were afraid of hostility on the part of rightist student groups, Paul Langevin had gone to Jeumont on the Belgian border to welcome him. A little before Paris, his wagon had been diverted and it was due to this circumstance that I owed this unusual encounter with him, at the Gare du Nord. It was also because of this discreet arrival that the next day's newspapers announced "Professor Einstein has Disappeared!"

In fact, he had been quietly driven to the German embassy, where he stayed, but his unique pair of shoes and his systematic refusal to wear a hat when he went out in the street — for he was totally opposed to being shut up in his room — was the talk of the town. It rained and the valet whose services were offered to Einstein insisted on keeping his shoes polished. The ambassador was worried about the effects of water and wind on the illustrious skull, but Einstein retorted that an abundance of hair protected his skull and besides that, the hair dried much more quickly than a hat ever would.

In the meantime, the newspapers attempted to turn public opinion in his favor. Everyone was interested in the famous theories of relativity — usually the less people understood of it, the more eager they were to get involved. Its author was granted the esteem of the Parisians even though he was a German because, as the astronomer Charles Noordmann (among others) recalled in *Le Matin*, "In the middle of the war, Einstein rejected Prussian militarism." No one pointed out, on the other hand, that he put French militarism on the same level. Hence, in addition to the rare specialists who were either enthused or bewildered by "relativity," everyone else in Paris who professed what they thought about it (or tried to make others believe that) hurried into an overflowing amphitheatre at the Sorbonne on March 31st to listen to Einstein's treatise and try to be interested in it. Now on the first of April, no one had to feign admiration for the speaker. He had conquered their hearts and minds, even if the notions of the spatial-temporal structure, the equivalence of mass and energy, of gravity and inertia, and other relativist subtleties, still remained just as incomprehensible, obscure, threatening or at the very least, mysterious. "Einstein," said *Le Figaro*, "has a handsome face, a high brow, hair that has been cut short since his last photographs and is naturally curly and peppered with silver strands, a mouth shadowed by a small moustache and eyes that are inspired rather than melancholic." The reporter added, with such evident surprise that it couldn't have been pretense, "This famous mathematician isn't at all austere, nor fierce, nor dry; on the contrary, his demeanor is soft and his smile is sweet."

In *L'Humanité*, Charles Rappoport showed the greatest enthusiasm, "Everyone had the impression of being in the presence of a sublime genius. As we saw Einstein's noble face and heard his slow, soft speech, it seemed as if the purest and most subtle thought was unfolding before us. A noble shudder shook us and raised us above the mediocrity and stubbornness of everyday life." A physical description followed, which was certainly not inferior to that of his colleagues with a particular accent on the eyes that had struck so much my childish imagination. "Oh, those eyes!" Rappoport exclaims. "Those who have seen them will never forget them. They have such depth! One might say that the habit of scrutinizing the secrets of the universe leaves indelible traces."

At that time Einstein was already forty-three years old. The earliest physical description we can find of him is by Maurice Solovine, who scolded him in a letter dated August 29, 1946: "You have written to me in a such polite manner — as if we weren't the best of friends, and hadn't done so many things together when we were young . . ."

Solovine, it seems, was Einstein's oldest friend; he was

the rigorous and competent translator of his work into French. "I was taking a walk in Bern one day during the Easter vacation of 1902, and I bought a newspaper," he relates, "I came across an ad that said that Albert Einstein, a former student at the Zurich Polytechnic School, gave physics lessons for three francs an hour. I said to myself, 'Maybe this man could introduce me to the secrets of theoretical physics?' So I went to the address that was indicated in the ad. I went up to the first floor and rang the bell. I heard a trumpeting 'Herein!' and then Einstein appeared. As his apartment opened onto a darkened hallway, I was struck by the extraordinary brilliance of his large eyes."

Were Einstein's eyes really a reflection of his soul? "The more I knew him," Solovine continues, "the more I found myself attracted to him. I admired his unusual penetration of the mind and his astonishing mastery of physical problems. He wasn't a brilliant orator and he didn't use dazzling images. He discussed subjects on a slow, uniform voice, but in a remarkably illuminating manner. In order to render his abstract thought more easily accessible, he occasionally borrowed from everyday experience." Then the relationship between teacher and student transformed itself into a solid friendship. "Our dinners were of an exemplary frugality. The menu usually consisted of sausage, a piece of Gruyère cheese, some fruit, a little pot of honey and one or two cups of tea. But we were overflowing with happiness. Epicure's words definitely applied to us: "Joyous poverty is a beautiful thing . . .''

We would only have a very incomplete vision of Einstein's physical characteristics without the account of Antonina Vallentin, one of the women who knew him best. "A young and yet an old man," she wrote, "(he) had regular features, full cheeks, a round chin, a male beauty which sprung from the hardships he endured, especially at the beginning of the century. A short nose, fine at the bridge, fleshy and sensual at the end. A thick mouth, very red under the black moustache, standing out against the pallid skin. At first glance, the lower half of the face would have belonged more to the category of sensual beings who always find reasons to love life and enjoy it. His round head was harmoniously joined to a powerful neck, sculpted as a column, with very white skin which sunburned easily. The large and, square shoulders belonged to a dock worker. A muscular body which later grew heavy, not fat like that of a sedentary person, unheedingly and flabbily, but with incoherence and regret like those retired from an active outdoor life such as captains or explorers in their old age. The eyes, however, disrupted that first impression — very dark eyes and very brilliant, like bulging spheres. The image went beyond a description of a handsome man, in love with existence. It had reached another world.

"A poet perhaps. Surely a musician. Those eyes, always brilliant and moist, most often sparkling with a lively fire, dreaming above the violin as if they were one with the sound. Moreover, his hands and the violin were also in complete harmony; large hands with sensual palms which slimmed towards the tapered fingers and rounded fingernails, the hands and the fingers of a musician. But above the soft and joyful gaze was the forehead. Not particularly high, but impressive by its size. Solid bone covered with neat skin, bone almost forming an arch between the rounded temples. He had an exceptional skull, the space under the cranial cavity would seem very vast even if his head were shaved. But then there was the mane, black in his youth, making him look as if he walked under a storm cloud. The hair was swept back from the forehead, wild and rebellious, as if animated by its own life. With the years, it grew spectacularly white. First it was just the two silver locks which sprang back from either side of the brow. Michelangelo's Moses. These silver streaks got more numerous, glittering among the dark locks, light and flying in the wind, and the colorful head sparkling with light. It could never be forgotten. He attracted every look. You could only feel uninteresting, and dull or foolishly embarrassed when you went anywhere at Albert Einstein's side.''

There was nothing equivocal in Einstein's relationship with Antonina Vallentin; nothing that could allow us to imagine that the painter's love has altered the model's portrait. Dimitri Mariano, who married Margot, the daughter of Einstein's second wife Elsa, is hardly less admiring or superficial in describing his father-in-law. He certainly cannot be accused of complacency because it seems that he had serious quarrels with the family which placed him at opposite ends with them and with Einstein especially. He says, ''The first thing however, that you notice about Albert is his powerful head. This power resides in the kindness of his expression which envelopes his whole being with a kind of radiant softness. His nose isn't Jewish, but large and fleshy. The severe bone structure which softens near the mouth, just at the chin, frankly, becomes feminine in appearance. He has the Jews' beautiful eyes. I've never met anyone with a head like that. Sometimes while looking at it, someone might say 'Yes, that's the head of Abraham of Ur in Chaldea, or maybe Jacob at the time when he saw the ladder reaching from the earth to the sky.' Because, as I gradually came to know him, in my estimation, his profile changed a hundred times. Sometimes it would become touching and disarming, like a little school boy, as he tugged at his curls, with a lost expression. Then, when all of his energy seemed to have been drained, his body collapsed and slackened in a completely feminine pose that is so often seen in tired people. At other moments, I saw him transported to an abstract, inaccessible domain; he would stand immobile like a monolith.''

In his first encounter with Einstein, at the famous ''Solvay Congress'' in 1927 when ''uncertainty'' and ''complimentary ideas'' were so heavily discussed, Louis de Broglie drew a similar sketch: ''I was very struck by the charm of his physical appearance, by the contrast of his expressions, sometimes dreamy and meditative, or other times lively and joyous.''

As for Romain Rolland, whose pacifist actions Einstein supported throughout the First World War, he wrote in his journal on September 16, 1915, the day after his visit, ''Einstein is still young, not very tall, with an imposing face, and an abundant mane; his hair is frizzy and dry, very black, peppered with gray, and growing back from a very high brow; his nose is fleshy and strong, he has a small mouth with fat lips, a small moustache that is cut short, full cheeks and a rounded chin. He speaks French with some difficulty, mixing it with German. He is very lively and jolly. He can't keep himself from making a joke out of the most serious thoughts.''

Finally, President Ben Gurion said: ''His face resembles that of God, as if the divine spirit were inside him, spreading as it does within those who approach this extraordinary divinity both human and cosmic.''

The attentive reader will have noticed certain discrepancies, indeed contrasts, in the physical descriptions of Einstein. They are inevitable because, in a human being, everyone sees more than what the physiological features reveal, due to complex psychological reasons. But psychology plays no part in regard to his clothing and here, all the opinions concur. It can all be summed up by this exclamation uttered by a professor at the University of Prague when Einstein arrived at his house for a formal visit: ''I could have sworn that it was an Italian virtuoso come to beg for assistance.''

Elsa wasn't the least bit elegant, but she did somewhat respect and maintain the common customs of the time and when Albert was preparing to leave to attend a congress or a series of lectures, she did her best to see that he would be dressed "like everyone else" and not draw attention to himself. But usually he came back in the same clothes that he'd been wearing the day he left, his suitcase arranged just as she had packed it. "Even worse," Elsa said, "one day he came back with his feet bare inside his shoes, and when we questioned him about it he answered, triumphant, 'Socks get full of holes much too quickly. I've discovered that they aren't absolutely indispensible and I'm not going to wear them so often from now on'."

After her divorce and the death of her mother, Margot, who lived with Einstein up to the time of his death, said, "In winter Albert dressed in an old brown leather jacket that we had given him as a gift several years before and which he wore constantly. He never changed clothes to welcome visitors. On cold or rainy days he added an English wool sweater. As for official dinners which he felt compelled to attend for one reason or another (but never out of "propriety") he had a formal suit, although a bit out of fashion, and he only wore a tuxedo for grand occasions, such as the acceptance of the Nobel Prize."

Antonina Vallentin adds; "He puts himself to much trouble and mischief to defend himself against the intrusion of the conventional in his existence. He only feels really at ease in a shirt largely opened on his powerful neck . . . He prefers what is familiar to him from long years of wear . . . to a material that is foreign to the touch; a bathrobe rull of holes seems much nicer to him than the new one he just received as a gift. Moreover, very elegant gifts had a way of disappearing eventually, carried off by some poor begger whom Einstein would have asked to go off discreetly, the package under his arm, in order to avoid the family's comments."

Einstein, in effect, never had a sense of propriety, and at every opportunity, he would flaunt it: "Can you imagine Moses, Jesus Christ or Gandhi with Carnegie's purse?" he said to an American association for the aid of Zionism which begged him to drop the subject in order not to upset their contributors. We know that he deliberately refused some fabulous appointments that Princeton offered, only accepting the ordinary salaries that didn't tie him down. He often demonstrated how man had converted money, a convenient system of exchange, into an evil entity, how it is so often found, in its various forms, as the basis of all kinds of conflict between individuals or groups, and how often it is the point of departure for all misery and injustice. Once he and Chaplin proposed to make a huge fire with bank notes and material possessions from all over the world, and have all peoples form a circle around it to celebrate their deliverance . . . Thus he gave a humorous twist to the ideas that he held close to his heart. He clearly understood that if he attempted to seriously carry them out, he would be accused of being a Utopian. "He is certainly a Utopian in this world," Father Teilhard de Chardin said, "but even outside the realm of physics, posterity will consider him an inspired innovator ahead of his time."

It was his efforts towards the creation of a world government after the second international conflict and his position on universal cooperation that often caused people to think him naive, if not utopian. He is a dreamer, Lunacharski, the head of the Soviet Delegation to the League of Nations, said in Geneva in 1932. "He is a naive dreamer. He fancies himself all-knowing because he understands mathematics, but he doesn't know men and their perversities."

There was at least some truth in that. Langevin, who also sat in the League of Nations, at Marie Curie's side, said "Einstein is convinced that man is capable of personal sacrifice provided he understands that what he does will further justice and reason." Langevin said this with the regret that it is not so. But Jules Mode found him less optimistic when the scientists welcomed him, as he then came out with this sentence, "Men are crazy." This was, it is true, in the fifties, right in the middle of the cold war, at the dawn of a "witch hunt" which certainly wouldn't spare him, in spite of his repute.

In Geneva his illusions seemed to be intact. Mme. Curie, with whom he loved to walk on the edge of the lake or go on excursions in the mountains, assures us that in developing the themes that were dear to him, his face lit up, he was "inspired." He asked to be reinstated in the international organization after having spectacularly resigned in order to protest against the occupation of the Ruhr which he thought was unjustified. Some said that "he was lowering himself." But perhaps he was never so great as in such circumstances — this was not the only one — where he sacrificed his own personal interests for a more general concern. "I salute Mr. Einstein," Bergson said in welcoming him back. "An old and new member at the same time: he was part of the commission, he left of his own free will, he asked to be reinstated; therefore his place belongs to him doubly."

Einstein smiled as if it were all quite friendly, only drawing a little more strongly on his pipe, with a sparkle of mischief in his eyes. But who knows what he was really thinking? Freud believed that he saw in him "Two diametrically opposed instincts: the instinct for conservation and procreation on the one hand, and the instinct for destruction on the other . . ."

Everything leads us to the conclusion that Einstein was never his own nor anyone else's fool. Professor Philippe Franck, the physicist who succeeded him in the chair he had occupied at the University of Prague, and who judges himself as being Einstein's "best scientific biographer," — Antonina Vallentin being undisputably his "best emotional biographer," — focused very clearly his attitudes while facing international scrutiny: "The confirmation of the Theory of Relativity awakened an immense interest in the public. Einstein ceased to be a man who only attracted scientists.

Just like a famous statesman, a victorious general or a popular actor, he became a public figure. He understood that along with the great renown he had acquired also came a great deal of responsibility. He felt that it would be egotistical and vain to simply accept the fact of being undisputed and to only pursue his research. He saw how the world is full of pain and thought that he knew several of the causes for this suffering. He also noticed that there were many people who pointed out these causes, but no one paid any attention to them because they weren't great men. He sensed that he was now a man who was listened to everywhere and that his duty was to be sensitive to these painful disgraces and to help eradicate them . . . He didn't feel that he was a political, social or religious reformer. In this regard he thought of himself just as any other cultured person. His advantage was that he could command public interest, and he wasn't one to be afraid of risking his great reputation, if necessary . . . In the days immediately following the [First] World War the essential problem . . . was naturally to prevent the advent of a similar catastrophy. The obvious means of attaining this goal was the development of international conciliation, the struggle against economical gaps, the fight in favor of disarmament and the energetic refusal of anything that tended to favor a militarist spirit . . . All these ideas appeared as obvious to Einstein as to many others. But he had more courage and more opportunity than the others to plead those causes . . ."

Jean Rostand said, "No one before Einstein had thus broken with the traditional secular way of thinking, no one had known how to liberate themselves from certain 'mental reflexes' that people thought were inscribed in the very organization of the species. No one before him had so strongly scandalized the so-called reason, which is imposed on common sense at such a great sacrifice. No one had submitted intelligence to such gymnastics. No one had abused this intelligence to such a degree in order to facilitate a better contact with the "real." This, written in praise of the relativist revolution, applies to all of Einstein's activity. The astrophysicist Evry Schatzmann, assures us that Einstein's greatness lay in his "never hesitating, when a cause seemed just to him, to defend it with word and pen."

A naiveté such as his was magnificent. Only children and those who have maintained that same childlike purity and balance are able to reveal the monstrous conventionalism of our civilization and attempt to suppress it.

On the occasion of Einstein's death, Francis Perrin wrote "Never did the old scientist, with his almost crazy stare, his childish smile and his imposing bearing feel very much at ease in the cruel and artificial world created by adults. His favorite companions were children, and perhaps his universal prestige lies partly in the fact that in our era we look back into childhood for faith in man's possibilities and its capacity to be astonished in front of all the world's marvels."

American journalists report, admittedly, different versions of the same anecdote: a little girl, his neighbor, would come and ask his help every time she had trouble finding the solution to an arithmetic problem, and Einstein answered the mother's apology in this way, "I've certainly learned more in my conversations with the child than the child has learned from me." He was genuine, firstly in his urbanity, and secondly in that he could get rid of people who bothered him without any formality.

"You will allow me to return, I hope, Professor?" he was once asked by a society lady who had managed, by intrigue, to make Elsa invite her to one of the musical evenings organized from time to time in their Berlin apartment.

"No," Einstein replied simply. And as Elsa protested after the departure of the mortified intruder, Albert, sincerely surprised, said to her, "But why should she come back? I really don't see the necessity!''

Ilsa, the eldest daughter, who tells this story, asserts that Einstein's interest — or his disinterest — in an individual never depended on the individual's title or social class, and a poor beggar could be retained for hours while an ''important personality'' might find himself rudely rejected. ''The tone he used in speaking to the official directors of the university,'' Franck said, ''was the same that he used to address his grocer or the woman who cleaned the laboratory . . . His attitude in relation to others was extremely free. He saw everyday facts in a rather comical light . . . his humor was quickly apparent . . . his laughter was a source of joy, a lively stimulant for those who were around him. Yet at times there was a hint of criticism which certain people found unpleasant. Important people often had no desire to belong to a world where ridicule — elevated to the scale of the greatest problems in nature — was reflected in Einstein's laughter. On the other hand, his personality was always pleasing to the people of a lower standing.''

More than others, he knew how to laugh at himself and his family always made up the chorus. There was an historical novel in which he was so obviously portrayed as Kepler that the greatest chemist Walter Nernst held the book out to him and said, ''This Kepler, it's you!'' Everyone was very amused, but the erecting of the statue at Riverside Church in New York was an even greater source of amusement. On the facade of this newly constructed church, Einstein discovered his effigy in stone in the middle of saints, kings and prophets, besides Archimedes, Euclid, Galileo, Newton, — and the only living one among them . . . and facing the abashed, if not scandalized pastor, he broke out in his heartiest laughter, saying: ''At the very most I might have imagined that one day I would be made a Jewish saint, but I never thought I'd become a Protestant saint!''

Whether it was a question of scientific work, of discussions or of collaboration in the most diverse fields, Einstein easily adapted himself, and did his best to maintain harmony. Marie-Antoinette Tonnelat, a great physicist wrote, "He had that virtue which only a very few attain, of bringing a way of thinking to life, of symbolizing scientific esthetics." Robert Oppenheimer, who was the director of the Princeton Institute when Einstein agreed to teach there, said "He was the greatest of all, and also the simplest." Niels Bohr, with whom he had gotten into an almost permanent controversy on the subject of philosophic interpretation of quantum theory, spoke with respect of his "infallible intuition," and preserved "the profound impression of a total absence in him of preconceived ideas." Frederic Joliot-Curie quoted his "astonishing broad scope." Henri Poincaré called him "the most original mind that I have ever known." The eminent American bacteriologist Simon Flexner, the first director of the New York Rockefeller Institute said, after their first meeting, "I was fascinated by his air of nobility, his charming simplicity of manner and his real humility. We strolled back and forth along the corridor of the Athenaeum (the University Club of the California Institute of Technology) for more than an hour. I explained, he questioned. A little after noon, Mrs. Einstein came to remind him that he had an appointment for lunch. "Fine, fine," he said amiably. "We have enough time. Let us talk a little longer." Flexner was only there to get his advice regarding the future of the Institute for Advanced Study, but having promised his assistance, Einstein didn't want to be disturbed by personal business. On the other hand, he detested putting himself before others. In the propaganda meetings in favor of Zionism (which he only joined after the Nazi persecutions, because he disapproved of any renewed nationalism), he generally was silent, seated close to Weizmann who called him "the Prophet of modern Israel."

Werner Heisenberg said that he was "extremely careful

not to shock anyone,'' although naturally he used all the resources at this disposal to attempt to convert his interviewer to his own views. The theorist in physics O. Costa de Beauregard wrote: ''During a stay at Princeton, I had the opportunity to have a conversation with Einstein on one of the great controversial topics between theorists in physics: hidden determinism or essential indeterminism of the laws of nature. I admit that I had a hard time departing from both my fascination with his very simple and very strong arguments and a vertigo from seeing his clear depth which seemed to exorcise the mystery. The mystery nonetheless remained, like an imperceptible coloration in the distance and sparkled like those objects which are foreign to us: the elementary constituents of matter. I left Einstein, a little drunk from having breathed in such a strong atmosphere, having bathed in such a brilliant light.''

To small-minded people, such as the deal of the University of Prague, who had this to say, ''You're not telling me that Einstein was a normal man? He was only an eccentric.'' But to great minds he always was seen in his true light. Mrs. Roosevelt called him ''a prestigious force of nature.'' Planck called him ''the Copernicus of the 20th century;'' and Von Laue, ''a revolutionary of human thought.'' For Schrödinger he possessed ''a genius superior to Newton's,'' and Max Born asserted, ''He would have been one of the greatest theorists in physics of all time, even if he had never written one line on relativity.''

Death did not frighten him. ''Einstein,'' his most remarkable collaborator, Leopold Infeld, said, ''wasn't afraid of death; he even laughed about it. When I went to visit him in the hospital where he was going to have an operation and I asked him about his illness, he answered me: 'The doctors themselves don't know!' And, breaking out into great laughter, he added, 'They'll find out from the autopsy'.''

Hans Reichenbach, professor of philosophy at the University of California, asked Einstein how he had arrived at the Theory of Relativity and was given this response: "Because I am firmly convinced of the harmony of the universe." He found this harmony not only in complex mathematics but also in music. Mme. Léon-Alvert Lasard, painter and designer, writes, "More than thirty years later I can hear the marvelous sounds that he knew how to draw from his instrument. He would have been a great artist. I see him today with his hair all messed up, dressed in a huge sweater, trousers with non-existent pleats, smiling at me while he signed some of the prints of the portrait which I made of him." Bernard Shaw assures us that "he resembled Beethoven more than Liebniz" adding "he's a musician in the guise of a scientist."

Emphasizing what H. G. Wells called Einstein's "subtle simplicity," the mathematician Jacques Hadmard writes "He reminded us of a visit that he made to our Paris apartment. He relaxed and played music and exhibited the most cordial good nature."

M. Georges Duhamel participated in this musical interlude. It is a strange thing," recounts the author of *Salavin*, "that I owe the pleasure and happiness of having met Einstein to music. During the war, I had learned to play the flute, and I owe wonderful hours of work and culture to that instrument. But I didn't play well enough to know the pure joy of playing solos. So I made up a musical group with a few friends. Thus I was invited by Jacques Hadamard, the illustrious mathematician, and a member of the Institute, to join a music ensemble. He announced to me that a German scientist named Einstein, and his friends were coming to join our group. He played the violin, and he took his place among the 'first violins' while, not far from him, I played 'first flute.' While counting the measures like a good student, I happened to raise my eyes above my music stand. I watched Einstein, listened to him, and I managed to distinguish him from the group. He was a good musician, as so many mathematicians are, playing neatly and precisely without ever showing off, never missing an entrance or a stroke. In the moments of silence he raised his handsome face, lighted with both intelligence and candor.''

Alas, this handsome face is no longer. Little by little, it changed, as with all beings who experience the relentless irreversibility of time. Charlie Chaplin depicted Einstein in his *Memoirs*, as ''the prototype of a German from the Alps in the most positive sense, jovial and friendly.'' Bertrand Russell states that he admired him ''even more as a man than as a scientist,'' the great Lorentz said that he ''would have liked to have had him as a son,'' and Paul Painlevé said of him ''he is the only man in the world that we cannot lose.'' Early on, his features began to grow old rapidly, to the point that, in 1948, a worried Antonina said sadly, ''His face is the face of a very old man. His shoulders are still robust, his bare neck round and powerful, but time has gathered deep furrows in his full cheeks, the folds which mark the corners of his lips fall low. Deep creases scar the great dome of his forehead. Before, they only appeared when he thought intensely, and when anger furrowed his brow, also when he laughed, but they used to disappear right away. Today they are permanently installed, irregular, afixed above the strong bridge of his nose. His temples are wrinkled with deep creases. However, the most moving change has occured in his eyes. It is as if all that is around his eyes has been burnt out by the intense regard and the deep brown fades into large mauve circles which sag above the cheeks. This brown and mauve stand out on the pale complexion just as the bluish lips do.''

''And yet,'' she adds, regaining hope or talking herself into it, ''if the eyeballs have taken refuge in the depth of their sockets, nothing could diminish and nothing has diminished the black fire of his pupils. This pale face is eagerly consumed by the inner soul, wrought with illness and suffering,

the hieroglyphics of all the torment having been handsome-
ly scratched into the flesh that weighs on the body, but a
force breaks through his eyes and triumphs over everything
that is declining.''

The terrible illness of his younger son, related to
psychiatry, had begun to depress him. "It torments him,''
Elsa said, frightened, ''He always aspired to be completely
invulnerable to everything that touched humanity. Actually,
he was much more vulnerable than any other man I knew
. . . But that situation was atrocious for him and he took it
with great difficulty. I no longer found the crazy sense of
humor in him, the taste for the unpredictable.'' Everyone
around him knew that he renounced what others call happiness and what he himself considered ''a foolish ideal.''
Along the same lines, he then attempted ''to renounce the
pain that isn't physical.'' He hadn't been able to, and if for a
long time he kept up the appearance of insensitivity and
detachment, his aspect now betrayed it. However the most
terrible ordeal was not caused by those closest to him.
''Einstein's gaze,'' Antonina Vallentin said, ''easily drifted
off into the distance, as if to assure himself of what still
lasted, of what had resisted the destructive will of man. This
abstract escape through the window pane was also an escape
from anguish, because anguish had survived with him in his
large room; it was within his reach. It lived beside him,
holding conversations with him. He spoke out loud, because
I found myself there by chance, as he often spoke to himself
in a low voice. He spoke freely of Hiroshima, of the un-
provoked horror that had been born that day. He spoke
of the course of destruction and of all that had been done to
aggravate it.''

Hadn't he, of whom Eve Curie said, ''He loved mankind
so much,'' endorsed their ruin in signing the appeal to President Roosevelt to put the techniques for nuclear destruction
in motion? On the twentieth of April, 1955, two days after

Einstein's death, Louis de Broglie wrote: "Albert Einstein not only had a great mind, but also a great heart, to which nothing that is human remained foreign. It is not at all astonishing; anxiety over fate and the future of men is not without its connections to the struggling over the enigmas of the physical world, because their roots are both plunged in the mystery of being."

Einstein had donated his body to the medical school connected with the Princeton Institute. In particular — he had discussed this problem many times with those who handled this kind of work — his brain was carefully dissected in an attempt to discover what anatomical-physiological "curiosity" might explain the psychological worth of the man who had dwelt there. There was no such thing. Upon first examination, Einstein's brain, of average size, did not differ at all from the brains of other men. "It did not differ from the anatomical-physiological point of view" — that, we must not hesitate to specify.

CHAPTER NINE

The Grandeur of Einstein

by LOUIS ARMAND
of the Académie Française

The richness of the texts published in this volume allows us to place Albert Einstein's accomplishments in the history of humanity. His uncontestable contributions to the progress of knowledge have clearly differentiated his brilliant work from mere passing phenomena. Through Einstein's efforts, human thought has crossed an irreversible threshold, that is the true criterion of progress; we will say "before Einstein and after Einstein," as we said "before and after Copernicus," "before and after Pasteur."

His genius manifested itself like a bright flash of light — several dozen pages, written at the age of twenty-five, marked the century. Certainly they met with skepticism, but Einstein was not preoccupied with the polemics which were provoked by his ideas. In any case, the skeptics did not prevent him from succeeding. He renewed the allegory of the triumph of Light over Darkness. The experimental verifications of his theories, in which everyone participated, appeared impossible because the corrections that his calculations brought to commonly observable phenomena were very weak. He felt no anxiety about these verifications, so the story goes, for the faith he had in his own reasoning had already led him to certitudes. His theories were recognized only when scientists learned how to observe particles the speed of which approached that of light and as they learned how to transform matter into energy. Until very recently, this happened only in the realm of dreams.

In today's world there is no question but that we calculate according to Einstein's theories.

Einstein originated a revolution of thinking and actually observed it come into being — for our era is characterized by its fast-moving pace. From 1905, the year that his first ideas on relativity were expressed, up until today, not only have the bomb and the atomic reactor been made but also machines for studying matter have passed from the laboratory scale to that of the giant factory, and radio-astronomy, unimaginable at the beginning of the century, has considerably increased the size of the observable universe. All of these areas were largely expanded due to Einstein's approach to mechanics, an approach which differed perceptibly from Newton's.

This same acceleration of history which allowed Pasteur and Newton to end their lives in great peace of mind as to the continued acceptance of their ideas caused Einstein to feel great anguish in the course of his life. His frustration lay in his having opened doors to areas that even he could not fully comprehend. His efforts in researching a single unifying theory, his reticence in regard to certain new ideas and the shift between today's advanced thinking and its heritage, demonstrate that all things merely rest on a given level, before soaring to new heights. This fact would lead to humility in someone other than Einstein. He had no need for it because he was steeped in it; humility was a part of his humanism.

Einstein's intellectual contribution is eminently synthetic, as was his exceptional openness of thought. He linked phenomena together and formulated connections, but these phenomena were already known and he only used existing mathematical tools. In other words — and this is the dominant trait of his work — his originality did not spring from new data extracted from experimentation or from a mathematical invention like the Fuchsian Functions discovered by Henri Poincaré (who also was interested in generalizations and syntheses). Rather, his genius led him to a new association of known facts and formulas, to a linking of the results of Michelson's experiment — which was, at that time, the only experiment which questioned former theories — to Riemann's geometric formulations and to the Levi-Civita equations. He was an architect of scientific thought; none of the elements were invented by him, but the construction was his, and it was marked by his spirit of simplification. He epitomizes one who discovers simple links in experimental data, and leaves his successors with the keys to open the many locked closets where Nature's secrets are hidden.

In our era of the explosion of knowledge and over-abundance of theories, it is significant that the accumulation of observations already necessitates new hypotheses, new simplifying formulas. Today we are sorely in need of a new Einstein to unravel all these entanglements. Such a feat calls for the strongest concentration of the mind that man is capable of summoning; this is the task of an individual rather than a team — as were Louis de Broglie's theories. It demonstrates that in our age of "group efforts," the attributes of the individual are still of the utmost importance in maintaining simplicity in our ever-changing world.

I would like to say that even more is required to succeed here: we need an individual, still himself, who is neither affected nor conditioned by the past; we need an imagination disposed towards acquired knowledge by disengaged from the established, long standing connections within this knowledge and not fearful of attacking indisputable ideas. This kind of creative imagination is just as necessary for the human sciences as for physics, because we must depend on this to disrupt the structures inherited from the past. Though technology has taken terrific strides in our era, nothing equivalent has developed in the domain of human behavior — such as politics or moral and ethical accomplishments. This has created an anxiety — producing imbalance which the civilized world simplistically attributes to technology, while it is truly ascribable to social structures that haven't "kept up." As the Pope declared to the United Nations, "It is not technology that is in question, but man." In effect, the responsibility as to whether technology be utilized for good or bad ends rests solely on the shoulders of mankind.

Einstein was no more a conformist in this domain than in pure science. He had reacted strongly against the anachronisms in society and the dangers they represent to the future of mankind. From all this he developed his positions against militarism, nationalism, violent revolution and the corruption of society by money. He used everything in his power to plead his causes. Due to his superior intellect, he exerted an unsolicited spiritual authority which was slightly diminished (oh, the irony of fate!) by the anachronistic aura of mystery surrounding him, for almost all of his admirers neither understood his work, nor appreciated his mind.

Alas, he was inflicted in this domain with the greatest conceivable disappointment: he, the German Jew, saw that his fame did nothing to diminish the anti-semitic crusade unleashed by his compatriots, a crusade that went so far as to condemn "Jewish science." He, the pacifist, was led to play an important role in the creation of the most murderous and inhuman of weapons — and then afterwards found himself powerless, in spite of his prestige, to keep it from being used. Such a fate reminds us of the heroes of ancient dramas, incapable, in spite of their obvious superiority in front of men, to divert the destiny of mankind.

It would be unjust to treat him as a Utopian because he believed in the League of Nations and pleaded in favor of a world government. Einstein was simply too far ahead of his time, as perhaps, an ancient Greek, who had foreseen the supression of slavery, might have been. It is rather more Utopian, in truth, to attempt to maintain or reinforce outdated structures or mentalities like certain forms of nationalism.

The great message that Einstein left is that, beyond yesterday's world, the rites and dogma of the past, an ideal can be applied to manners of thought and action and turned towards the future without losing its force. Of this, Teilhard de Chardin said "Even outside of physics, posterity will consider him (EINSTEIN) an inspired precursor." We can nurture this ideal with the present and the future as much as with the past; knowledge can be associated, in this way, with faith, and both are equally as important as he himself insisted: "Science without religion is lame, religion is blind without science."

Although an anti-patriot and non-religious (in the sense that these terms contain no value judgments) he was, like Newton whom he admired so much, a great mystic. We can remember these comforting words, coming from a man so much at home in the intellectual world, "The mystical feelings are the most beautiful that we can experience."

Thus his mastery of rational thought never prevented him from being sensitive to human warmth nor from recognizing the supremacy of that which transcending man and his mind, exists without surrendering its secrets. His evidence — and what evidence! — confirmed that, if certain individuals dominate others in the research of the "how" of the world, all are equal in ignorance of the "why." There, we find the most convincing reason to unite in common humility.

INVENTORY 1983